Illustrated by
MICHAEL BELL

PARISH PUMP
C. Gordon Glover as 'Julian Grey'

KINETON · THE ROUNDWOOD PRESS · 1975

By the same Author:
Cocktails at Six, 1934 (Bles)
Week-end in Town, 1934 (Bles)
Bolero, 1936 (Cassell)
Family Gathering, 1937 (Cassell)

Published by The Roundwood Press (Publishers) Limited,
Kineton, Warwick, England.

Set in 'Monotype' Van Dijck series 203, and printed by Gordon Norwood
at The Roundwood Press, Kineton in the County of Warwick, England
and bound by Eric Neal, Welford, Northampton.

Made and printed in England

The material contained in this collection of essays first appeared in *The Country Gentleman's Magazine*. The author and publishers wish to acknowledge their gratitude for permission to reprint them in this book.

CONTENTS

PREFACE

WHEN I TOOK over the editorship of *The Country Gentlemen's Magazine* in January 1969 I invited Gordon Glover to write a series of essays describing life as it is today in a village not more that 50 miles from London. I gave him a completely free brief. I can do no better than quote from the first of these 'Parish Pump' articles:

"Over the past thirty years the village, in the swing of the seasons and the winds of change, is not what it used to be. Once upon that time ago there were paraffin lamps, well-water, a ford over Winterstream where now there is a bridge, and an Elsan privy in a brick box hard by the back door. Now, at the turn of a tap and the click of a switch there is instant amenity. But the paraffin lamps, after a spell in the wilderness, have modishly returned, and to live in the country is still vivid and even adventurous.
Life in cities, however prinked up with footlights, trendy Trattorias, surges of symphony orchestras under visiting conductors, the King's Road, Chelsea on a Saturday morning, boutiques in byways and mondaine goings-on in basements is grey and uniform when regarded on a day-to-day basis. There is lacking the dawn-to-dark warmth and waspishness of rural living where every face, nice or nasty, is familiar and has a name to it. Urban friends on week-end visits frequently return to their burrows exhausted and bewildered by the intensity of the climate of sleepy-hollow."

As a B.B.C. colleague, Arthur Phillips, said in his tribute to Gordon, "to travel with him was a joy and an education." Through

Gordon's eyes the country took on another dimension. A lane of beech trees for him became "a herd of elephants standing sentinel in pools of gold." His concern for country life and his ability to conjure up the spirit of it never left him; and, indeed, he was writing a 'Parish Pump' article for *The Country Gentleman's Magazine* on the very day of his death. He had a love of rich words and though his radio programmes were inevitably given to a certain amount of nostalgia, he could still smile upon some of the transformations that have overtaken the English countryside since the war.

Let 'Parish Pump' become his fitting memorial.

NOEL CURRER-BRIGGS

Write when there is something that you know: and not before: and not too damned much after.

ERNEST HEMINGWAY

LIFE IN A village is life which is always recognisably seen to be being lived. Everyone knows everyone else. If they don't, then they make it their business to put this wrong to rights as soon as may be possible. The average village – and most villages are that – is a private microcosm of human fears and aspirations, prides and prejudices, likings and loathings, industry and indolence. It is all too easy to romanticise, and here and there maybe I have succumbed, as the mood has taken me, to the temptation of roses ever blooming fresh around the door, and the wind blowing always sweet on the heath, brother.

But oh! brother! while both be there, the first are often tattered, tatty and torn, and the second icily forlorn. Like people, warts and all. Not all village ladies are wholesome as cottage loaves, nor village men prototypes of rough-hewn rustic probity. Images of the homespun syndrome there certainly remain, though slowly on the decline. 'Grand old characters' are to be found, of course, although many so-called are bigots and bores. Nor are the crab-apple jelly-making ladies of the W.I. totally pure of heart and bereft of guile. In any event they properly resent the notion that all they do is make crab-apple jelly and Victoria sponges. Like everything else in England's green and pleasant land the Women's Institutes have undergone the winds of generally progressive change.

If there are more bankers and stockbrokers than fairies at the bottom of country gardens, they again are a wind of change and not to be disregarded in the pattern of village life and living.

If in some of these brief musings I may be accused of putting over-emphasis upon the part in village affairs played by the village pub, then I have done so without shame. I would hold a village without a tavern to be like Hamlet without the Prince. The pub is the mainspring of the rural timepiece, the beating heart of the matter.

In my own village I have lived, still as a 'foreigner', and a Scottish one at that, for half an average lifetime. I have kept eyes and ears alert, and present these reflections in the hope that such findings of eye and ear may prove acceptable.

Though there remain still many pastures of ignorance, with a new one to be explored and astonish every day, I believe that I have written about something which I at least claim to know.

But not, I trust, too damned much.

JULIAN GREY

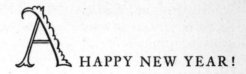

CHAPTER ONE

A HAPPY NEW YEAR!

VERY WELL, THEN, let us in this winter season be briefly bewitched or bedevilled, by the opposing spirits of Bob Cratchit and Ebenezer Scrooge, by Christmas all too presently passed, and a heady cup of kindness taken for Auld Lang Syne. 'A guid New Year tae yin an' a',' and 'Ding Dong Merrily on High' from the bell tower of the Parish Church ringing out the old year and ringing in the new across the cold greensward where stands the Parish Pump.

That symbolic stump of ancient ironmongery has but recently been repainted by a parishioner (unpaid!), and looks as though it had been donated to the village as a Christmas gift from an over-stocked Folk Museum. It is no longer the open-air Forum for village wives with their buckets and pails, although the shades of them still flit about it at the end of memory lane. And the shade, too, of bachelor Bert Billings who, corduroys tied with twine below the knees and looking like something which had crept from the stack-yard of Cold Comfort Farm made it his daily act of neighbourliness to fill, and deliver, the evening pail of water to the shady lady who, with no resident husband, lived with her four children in a now long demolished moss-grown hovel by the banks of the brook. The lady's garden was a native bushland of dock, nettle, thistle, ground-elder and mallow whose candy-striped blooms standing alongside the yellow roughage of ragwort in summertime did bestow upon the jungle some pretention of being a flower garden.

It was up the narrow path through this wilderness that Bert, pail in hand, trudged upon each evening's errand of mercy to the lamplit burrow in which the shady lady was well content to receive him.

But there was another man in her life who, apart from one or two unannounced three-day descents upon her throughout the year, kept his safe distance in Saltash where he pursued some kind of occupation within sight of the great bridge of Isambard Kingdom Brunel. Husband? Who knew? The shady lady's own bridge across the brook was constructed of a few boards and a handrail. It was upon the hovel side of this in the half-light of an April evening that Bert Billings with water pail in his hand was met by the person-from-Saltash with a wood chopper in his.

From a window below the moss green sparrow-pitted thatch the children set up their squalling chorus of apprehension, since the person-from-Saltash had clearly looked very well upon the wine when it was red. The shady lady let fly her own squeals of anguish from the open doorway, that time wood chopper met water pail mid-bridge. Bert Billings, temporarily shielded, took a backward step of retreat, held his ground and turned defence into offence by discharging the whole of his liquid artillery over the person-from-Saltash. Need it be said that pail and chopper fell into the brook in the first shock of close encounter, followed in seconds by the arm-flailing contestants, one to scramble up one slippery slope towards the new season's ragwort, the other to take the opposite escape route?

Strangely enough, the pair were to be seen the following day all amity and concord over pints of Bitter-and-Burton in *The Star and Wheelbarrow*.

Just one sweet little posy gathered from the banksides of memory lane.

Always look forward, and never look back. Nostalgia is fungoid and negative. Is it? The stuff of it was real enough at the time, and forward-looking *can* be as ephemeral as pie-in-the-sky. That long ago, red-blooded, water-loaded rumpus by the brookside in all its coarse comicality was, as it's said, 'for real'. As real as that last day in the old year 1936 when the pair of us stood by four oil lamps in that first cottage of ours near the Parish Pump awaiting, long over-due, the arrival of the removal men. It had been snowing for most of the day, and in the five o'clock darkness the snow was still lightly falling.

Were we out of our minds ever to have come to this heaven-forsaken hole among the by-roaded hills, having decided to *live* in it? No thought of country living had been further from my mind when in the July of that same year, homing Londonwards at leisure and deliberately through unknown byways, I rounded a road bend and there before me, surrounded by a gossiping posse of countrywomen upon the green stood the Parish Pump. And beyond it in the bee-loud glade of high summer stood the straw-roofed, whitewashed cottage with the board before it proclaiming FOR SALE.

What's more, there were roses round the door – Paul Scarletts – the whisper of the shallow brook over the ford, the muzzy scent of honeysuckle against the clap-boarded walls of the village shop where I had stopped, and, for good measure, a country clergyman almost straight from Trollope, emerging from that very shop.

'A beautiful day, sir', said the parson, 'I see you're admiring our village. Peaceful spot, isn't it?'

'Indeed it is', I answered.

'If you're thirsty, sir', said the parson, 'I recommend the beer in our Inn just down the road.'

'Thank you', said I. 'I'll go and try it.'

'I would join you were I able', replied the parson, 'but I am expecting the doctor at midday to have a look at this', and he removed a sun-bitten old Panama hat from his gossamer-covered skull. He disclosed an angry looking purplish lump. 'I was practising mashie shots in the meadow this morning', went on the reverend gentleman, 'when an unpardonably awful slice came straight back at me from an ash tree and near as nothing knocked me out. Serve me right. A *dreadful* shot. Ah, there's the doctor driving up to the Rectory now.'

Into *The Star and Wheelbarrow*. The tick-tock tick-tock of a pendulum wall-clock. A caged grey parrot which gave the only 'Hullo' across the muffling silence which always falls among the occupants of village tap-rooms at the appearance of an instantly suspect stranger.

Was it the honeysuckle scent, the roses, the bees, the parson or the second cool, lightly heady pint in *The Star and Wheelbarrow* which led me to the front door of that Cottage For Sale and, within ninety minutes of first sighting the Parish Pump, making the greatest decision of a lifetime? I shall never know, but, without even consultation with the life partner, I made it upon one faraway summer's day.

It was all very different in the freezing snowfall of that New

Year's Eve, and would the removal men ever arrive? A log fire burned in the open hearth. Bare walls, bare-boarded floors, uncurtained windows, and the owls hoo-hooing through snowfall to the last night of the old year. What a night upon which to implement the decision of a lifetime! Twenty five poundsworth of bathroom plumbed against the arrival of mains water two years away: the cottage wired in readiness for when electricity would be turned to fact beyond vague hope; and the furniture, two deck-chairs and an empty crate. But, down at *The Star and Wheelbarrow* a featherbedded iron bedstead upholding a pair of stone hot water bottles, and, in an open grate, a fire of blazing coals provided by, but undemanded from, that hospitable innkeeper.

This is nostalgia, and I'm glad of it. Glad to remember at this so recent turning of a later year that night of lamplit yesterday when the clouds cleared, the snow no longer fell and under the prickly shine of the winter stars the pantechnicon which had been two hours deep in a by-road ditch came bumbling down the lane to stop outside the cottage whose FOR SALE sign had been all honey bees and roses in deep July.

By lamplight and beer-bottled candle flame an empty box among the freezing hills became a home. Ah, me! the good cheer and the near-midnight expertise of those removal men. The unpanicky, slow-moving miracle of huge bedsteads being manhandled up narrow cottage stairs. Oh, yes, it had been a difficult day for them – a flat tyre at its beginning, a brake failure somewhere around Watford, two hours in a repair shop, the blizzard, the darkness in the by-road ditch. Oh, yes, they'd got to get back to London after checkout here in the backwoods – they were off to Bristol on New Year's Day!

At ten minutes before midnight the next-door neighbour, hurricane lamp in hand, bade us and three removal men present ourselves for welcome to the New Year and the village before the stroke of twelve. Mince pies, Highland Malt whisky, lamplight and an aura of love. Our host was Scots. 'A guid new year tae yin an' a'' cried he, wrinkled as a walnut and sentimentally bottled to boot!

It was a New Year's Eve ever to be remembered, that first of all by the Parish Pump, warm in the first hours of New Year's Day as the firelight flickering upon the ceiling of that pre-war tavern bedroom, and the flubsy hills and vales of that unforgotten featherbed.

4

5

CHAPTER TWO

THINGS WAS DIFFERENT THEN

'AR, BUT MIND ye – things was different in them days. . . '

They certainly was! But it didn't need these words from Alfred Porson, aged habitué of *The Star and Wheelbarrow*, to convince me of the fact. Even though he did add: 'Whoi, when fust oi come into *The Star*, and quoite a lad I was, they give 'ee a clay poipe free with the beer, that's what they give 'ee, if ye was short of a poipe, that was.'

'Free, you say, Alfred?'

'Aye, free. But things was different in them days.'

I have before me pictorial evidence that things was different in them days. Not that even Alfred Porson was around in 1840 when this water-colour drawing of the then very Early Victorian village was most eloquently painted by a young lady, daughter of the then Rector of the Parish. Young ladies of the nineteenth Century, all untutored, seemed naturally born to the skills of 'ladylike accomplishment' – fine needlework, crochet, the writing of verses and, not least, that most English of aptitudes, the talent for painting in water-colour.

Here, with the still standing Parish Pump of today very much in the foreground, is a beguiling example of that talent, an evocation of a summer's day in 1840. The Parish Pump, now only a cast iron pillar upon its little green, has a long handle. A village matron with sun bonnet and pail in hand stands close by. Behind her where now a road bridge crosses the brook there is a ford, its bankside dabbled with white ducks, and beyond that the green which still slopes gently up towards the south side of the church. Three little girls in pinafores would seem to be making daisy-and-buttercup chains upon the green, for it is freckled with the pretty things. Today there is no lychgate, but lo! and behold, there *was* then, ridged with red tiles and, close beside it, stood the figure of an old man in a linen smock with a frill of white whiskers around his chins. What's more, the church, its roof slated today, was also covered with rippling peg-tiles. And just to the left of the south porch, and above it, the window of what would seem to be a little room of some kind. There is a chimney-pot left of the window.

Whatever sort of snuggery was this within the fabric of the church walls? Was it a cosy carpeted den in which the Rector, seated before a bright fire, could think brown thoughts in a brown study? Prepare his sermons? Get away from wife and family?

Maybe the Rector's daughter, the young water-colourist, had just drawn in the little room for fun since there is no evidence in today's fabric that it ever existed.

Rector, family, flower-picking little girls and sunbonneted matron by Parish Pump are long laid in earth. But there they were, together with the white-whiskered parishioner in the smock, in a scene more vividly warmhearted than any which could be conveyed by the camera's eye. I can hear the ripple of the brook over the shallow ford and the laughter of the children, and I seem to scent the buttercups and daises.

Things was different in them days. And were any of the persons assembled, I wonder, ancestors of Alfred Porson in his corner of *The Star and Wheelbarrow*? The churchyard is full of Porsons, and four of them still breathe the air about the Parish Pump today. Old Alfred and his Missus, Angie, son Dave and daughter-in-law May.

Dave is a broad oak tree of a countryman, carpenter, joiner, one-man-band of a jobbing builder – owner of a workmanlike pick-up and a Mini for taking May out for a ride-around Sundays, or summer evenings. Dave has left the village only once in his life, to exchange the waters of the brook for the sands of Alamein and the slaughter-house of the Anzio beach-head. These experiences did not incline Dave towards further foreign travel. A Union Jack and a piece of canvas lettered 'Welcome Home Dave' greeted Dave when he returned in his demob. suit. Within the week he was back in over-alls and the workshop which father Alfred had kept going through the war years. 'Porson and Son' was in being again.

Good peasant stock, the Porsons, generations of them, knowing their places, keeping their station, being christened, married and finally laid to earth within the precincts of the Church of Saint Mary the Blessed Virgin upon the summit of the Green. Things was different in them days, but it was clear, even when he was at school, that Dave Porson's son Clive was going to change them. Not he for the good old ways of the good old days. To Law School went young Clive, thereafter to be articled to the long-established firm of Bradberry, Hucklidge and Hooke of Steepleborough.

The Porsons, Dave and May, were openly proud of this professional 'ascent of man' as evidenced by son Clive. Old Alfred, equally openly, was appalled. The very idea! What was young fellers coming to these days? Whoi things was different in them other days. What was the matter with a young feller turning his hand to a proper man's 'wuk'? A grandson of his 'going fer the Law'!

'Oi never have trusted they lawyers, and I never will, that oi'm telling ye. All they wants is yer money, and to think that a grandson o' moine. . .'

On an August day young Clive, Junior Partner in the firm of Bradberry, Hucklidge and Hooke, was married to Annabelle Hooke, daughter of Jason Hooke of Steepleborough. And the Hookes *could* afford a carriage *and* a marquee in the garden of their small Georgian house in the village of Honeywell near Steepleborough. But with decent deference to the long Parochial lineage of the Porson family in *this* village the courteous Hookes – having left the appropriate suit-case around *this* Parish Pump – had Annabelle published in the Banns as 'Spinster of this Parish.'

'Marry'n beneath him, that's what he's a-doing of, young Clive', was old Alfred's pronouncement concerning the whole affair. But he had to face up to the grey tophatted impact of the winds of change, the New images of democracy – the peasants 'thinkin' they was betterin' theyselves' by marrying into the gentry. That was, if they lawyers fancied theirselves gentry, which they wasn't, come to think on it. But the Hooke family, being very true 'gentry', were graciously uncondescending to the Porson family and thought that much good could be done to each family's blood by this union between land and law. But, for their daughter's sake, they insisted that she be sent off in style.

It was not, mind you, *all* grey toppers, and most certainly not for old Alfred with gold albert across his Sunday suit weskit, and that was that. But the memory remains with me of oak tree Dave, proud father of the groom, looking like John Bull himself, stream-lined into the current decade, calmly splendid in striped pants, tails and grey topper, standing with the family group outside the south porch of the Church of the Blessed St. Mary, back of the green by the Parish pump – back of the green where the little girls had made daisy chains in 1840 and an ancient man in a smock had stood by the lychgate.

Later on, among the canapés and the Krug and the carnations in the marquee, I spoke with old Alfred for whom a seat in the breeze had been found. He seemed mellow and at his ease, though the top of a cottage loaf with bread, cheese and pickled onions, washed down with a pint of mild and bitter, would have been more to his fancy than sniblets of smoked salmon and fingers of asparagus cushioned in thin brown bread.

'Oi must say' said old Albert, 'as they seem real nice folks, and that oi'd never've believed, being lawyers loike. Just fancy – our young Clive looking easy as you please with such folks. Mind ye, when I wed my old Angie it wor'n't loike this But a hoigh of it we had in the Church Hall, what with the dancing and fiddle playin' and that. But things was different in them days.'

'And they're different in these. Alfred.'

'You never said a truer word, sir – never said a truer word.'

For only the second time in our thirty-plus years of neighbour-liness had Alfred Porson called me 'Sir'. Just what was the slightly wrong note here? It would be 'Julian, mate' again on the morrow.

It had been a great day!

CHAPTER THREE

ORNING SURGERY

IT WAS MORNING Surgery a little while back in the larger village which rambles along the B road midway between the Parish Pump and the market town of Steepleborough. Monday *morning* Surgery at that, which is always the busiest of the week, as residents of hamlets for miles around come to proclaim their distempers to one of the four doctors who are part of what is very properly known as The Partnership.

We perch around the waiting room walls on hard and brightly coloured chairs of some adroitly fabricated substance. We give little sniffs and low coughs from time to time and shuffle our behinds on the seats of our little yellow and scarlet chairs. Two ladies, side by side across a corner of the waiting room, communicate in audible undertones about the nature of their sufferings and the blessed release from *his* of some old countryman unknown to the rest of us who was laid in earth a week ago Friday.

We leaf listlessly through the pages of old Country Lives, dog-eared glossies, Horses and Hounds, The Fisherman, and, indeed, The Country Gentlemen's Magazine, for this is, let it be known, a countryside surgery, and, apart from the odd feminine glossy and some multicoloured comics for the kids, the accent on the reading matter offered is firmly countrysided.

While we are leafing we are also, of course, listening for the sudden electrical click followed by the rasping of a definitely dated old non-intercom speaker as one of the four Partners in tones of distort and strangulation addresses the company thuswise: 'Mr Podger in Dr. Carpenter's office, please – Mr Podger in Dr. Carpenter's office.' Click-Out. No 'Roger-and-Over'. Mr Podger, a parishioner of Parson's Green, says: 'Eh? What was that?', and then, realising that wall speakers don't go in for dialogue, rises to his feet and shuffles out of the door towards his fate or fortune.

The waiting room whisperings, shufflings and page rustlings were now broken by the bearlike growlings of the ancient man seated upon the plastic perch next to mine. Vaguely I recognised him as something, someone, whom I had known long ago, not a resident around our own Parish Pump, but very surely a someone with whom over the years I had rubbed shoulders in the Rural District.

'Loike as not ye'll not remember me, Mr Grey, sir, but I knows you all right. Used to see ye in *The Star* years ago when I come over to see my sister as lived near enough alongsoide of ye. Ye'll remember old Doctor Wilkinson, I daresay, sir?'

'Why, yes, do I *not*? Who'd forget Doc Wilkinson? One of the old school, he was . . .'

'Oi wonder what old Doctor Wilkinson'd make of all this malarky, Mr Grey, sir, eh? Couldn't see *'im* being bothered with it. A *real* doctor 'e was and no mistake. All they give ye now is five minutes and tablets. Doctor Wilkinson, 'e give ye *proper* medicine, real physic it was, and you allus 'ad to shake the bottle. *These* days it's just 'angin' about and tablets.'

In the year 1905, I read recently, there was a solemn and serious threat in Imperial Russia by all physicians in rural districts to – yes, *strike*! An English man of letters granted the privilege of an audience with Leo Tolstoy mentioned this seemingly unseemly action to the author of *War and Peace*.

'All the better', said Tolstoy.

'But then', replied the visitor, 'all the peasants will be without medical help.'

'So much the better. Forty or fifty years ago when I was young there *were* no doctors among the peasants, and the peasants got on very well without them.'

When first I came to live alongside the Parish Pump before the Second World War both peasants and literary and other eccentrics who had chosen Mother Greenfields as a way of life would have got out rather worse *without* Doctor Wilkinson. Within a month of our settling in there was a thundersome knock on the front door, and there stood a rocky-looking man in a well cut, hairy tweed suit with, upon his head, one of those blunt stiff hats which looked like the offspring of a topper and a bowler. The hat was of a warm-hearted snuff colour.

'Mr Grey?' said the caller, 'Glad to meet you. I thought I'd call in passing. My name is Wilkinson, Doctor James Wilkinson. Edinburgh Faculty of Medicine, 1901. May I come in?'

Of course he came in. I introduced Dr. Wilkinson to my wife and two year old son. 'Madam', said he, 'Your servant. As for this young man he looks well nourished enough to me, but don't keep him short on the malt.' The Doctor swept his eyes critically around our little sitting-room. 'Hm' he said, 'You've got some nice things. Inherited, I'd say. Young people in your profession couldn't afford a Georgian piece like that lowboy there. You're writers, I'm told. No money in writing. Never mind, I'll take a chance and take you on. That's to say, if Charlie McGregor hasn't got his foot in first.'

We assured Dr. Wilkinson that we knew no Charlie McGregor, be he Mr, Dr. or Peer of the Realm. Dr. Wilkinson said that he and Dr. Charles McGregor were the best of friends and colleagues, and that, as men of medicine, there was little to choose between them. 'But', he added, 'when new people arrive Charlie's generally a step ahead of me in making his number known. Not that we *tout* for patients. Most unethical. But we like to look over the potential.'

Sounds strange today, doesn't it? Doctors *seeking* custom rather than putting up the 'House Full' notices. But that was the way of it in the late thirties.

'Would you care for a drink, Doctor?' I asked with decent temerity.

'If the stuff comes from North of the Border', said our new-found medical adviser, 'I accept with pleasure. Treated with the respect it deserves, the best physic there is. Thank you, Mr Grey.'

'Ah', said the old joker next to me in the surgery waiting room of today, 'Friend to everyone, was old Doc Wilkinson. Allus come out to ye, 'e would.'

Once, indeed, Dr. Wilkinson *did* 'come out' to an aged pair of parishioners living out in the sticks at the end of a long wintry lane. It was the milkman on his every-other-day delivery who hammered on the Doctor's door at 6.30 of an icy morning, saying, 'Sorry, Doc, but I thought you should see this. Found it stuck in a milk bottle what I picked up outside of the old Cattermoles' place. "Send for Doctor Urgent", it says, "Alf's taken bad". And that's two days ago, Doc.'

Hurling on woollen socks, woollen dressing-gown over pyjamas, topcoat over all, and gumboots, the Doctor set forth. Not, as you might imagine from all this, in a pony and trap, but in a ten year old $4\frac{1}{2}$-litre Bentley, fabric body, racing green, bonnet held down by huge leather strap, always open to wind and weather. A demon for fast motor cars was Doc Wilkinson.

Arrived 7 a.m. at the Cattermole cottage, he was warmly greeted by the couple who were breakfasting before a roaring fire.

'Whoi, Doctor, this *is* a surprise. Noice to see ye. Ye'll take a cup of tea and a warm, will ye?'

'But', said the Doctor, 'I have this note. Perce the milkman gave it to me this morning.'

'Oh, that!' said Ada Cattermole, 'That was writ two days back, and Alf's better now, isn't yer, Alf? But it was nice of ye to call, Doctor.'

Dr. James Wilkinson, known to us in time and the beaten paths of friendship as 'Jamie' was unforgettable. He was rough, kindly, shrewd and sometimes straight rude. 'Mrs Grey', he once bawled at my wife on a winter's afternoon when she was taking the then three year old heir for a laneside ramble, 'Mrs Grey, you should be damned well ashamed of yourself exposing the child to a north-easter on a winter's day without adequate clothing. See he's properly wrapped up next time we meet.' And away he boom-boomed in the open Bentley, most improperly wrapped up himself.

Doctor Wilkinson drank tap-room ale in taverns for miles around, just, he said, to 'keep an eye on some of my panel patients'. He was president of his village Football and Cricket Clubs. Cricket at the age of over sixty he still doggedly played, wearing lightweight brown shoes. He was an amateur actor of decent distinction. He was, let's face it, well beyond the 'tonsils-out-on-the-kitchen-table' days, but he could very surely have done the deed if needful. 'Physician and Surgeon' read the bright brass plate outside his small Georgian residence. I once went to him with an impacted great toe. '*Hallux Rigidus*, that's what you've got, old son', he said.

'Can you sort it out with a bit of minor surgery, Jamie?' I asked.

He fixed me with that straight blue eye of his. 'There is no such thing, my dear Julian, as "minor surgery". All surgery is surgery and important when it works. I can take your toe off if you ask me to, but I wouldn't advise it. Damned unbalancing with a big toe

14

short. Hobble around. It'll probably sort itself out in time.'

And it did.

Dr. James Wilkinson was in his early seventies when he decided to retire and go fishing. The War was over, and so was the old green Bentley. His brand new Jaguar soft-top was among the first to come off the post-War assembly line. Before he left to retire into Wales between two salmon rivers he called personally – in the Jaguar – upon every one of his patients to say 'Goodbye.'

Many of us wept to see him go. Truly wept. When over fifteen years later we learned that 'Old Doc Wilkinson' had fallen finally asleep on the bankside of a roaring Welsh salmon river, the now 'old Jag' behind him, we smiled and raised distant glasses to the memory of a memorable man.

There are, of course, men who will be remembered among the four who are now, with their Monday-packed waiting room, the new style 'Partnership'. These words from the Parish Pump do not flout the new and overpraise the old. Times and Doctors-Within-Them change.

But there will never be, or can ever be, another Doc Wilkinson.

CHAPTER FOUR

AR RELIEF

'TO BE QUITE HONEST with you', said the stranger in the deerstalker perched by his pint at the far end of the bar of *The Ancient Shepherd*, 'I rather like it.'

Three natives of the adjoining Parish in which *The Ancient Shepherd* stands, plus the landlord, turned, jaws dropped in disbelief, upon the foreigner who had uttered this heresy.

'*Like* it?' cried one, 'You – you *like* it?'

'What on *earth* do you find to like about it?' asked another.

'Well', replied the visitor, outnumbered and undismayed 'I think it's bright and cheerful, and it lets you know where you are. After all', he added, 'we do live in a changing world, you know, and this is just another symptom of change. We can't go through life standing still you know. No – I may be unpopular, but I like it.'

So he liked it, did he, this, this . . . Who was he, anyway? Most probably, we privily thought, a snooper from Big Brother Brewery who had, willy nilly, torn down the quiet old sign which had proclaimed with decent black lettering upon a primrose-coloured background the words *The Ancient Shepherd*, and substituted for it this flaring plastic obscenity, a moulded monstrosity of raised white lettering upon a new background whose colouring suggested that somebody had sicked up a surfeit of buttered eggs.

The Ancient Shepherd, I may say, is very ancient indeed, an old village inn in an old English village, an inn which, I may add, had until some fifteen years ago a silver-grey flooring of flagstones in its tap-room, two inglenooks for the comfort of ancient men and a pair of high-backed, draught-protecting settles. Its walls were – and are – of lath and plaster about a timber frame and an overall air of being what it truly was, a no-nonsense-about-it country pub.

'*Plus ça change, plus c'est la même chose.*'

Not with this new image, it isn't. Just right for something in red brick on the street corner in some semi-suburban hinterland, or to raise the spirits of a parched traveller in the Libyan Desert – where the sign would out-eye-catch the sun. But, together with 'Toilets' in buttered egg ochre at the back of the car park, really not on for *The Ancient Shepherd*. But there it is, an earnest, proclaims Big Brother Brewery, of many similar signs to come. This, irrespective of the style of premises, is to be his recognisable image throughout the length and breadth of the land wherever he serves his devitalised beer to the already numbed consumers. The consumer's heart is assumed to be gladdened by this plastic gallimaufrey by harbour fronts, riversides or ancient East Anglian market towns where the pargetting of house walls proclaims the days of jolly waggoners. Many a *Jolly Waggoners* tavern will, doubtless, soon be seen from a great distance, for this is the thinking of powerful, impersonal men in the hiding of high places.

'You seen the new sign down *The Shepherd*?' ask regulars in our own *Star and Wheelbarrow*, 'half blinds you, don't it?'

'Someone wants his head tested', observes another, 'Suppose it'll be our turn next.'

And I very well daresay that it will, since any strange car any day may contain a prospecting party from the self-same Brewery Chain which has vilified the poor old *Shepherd*. The Ancient Shepherd was, as they say, 'done up both inside and out scarcely a year ago.' Quite respectably, really, although its tenants who requested matt-painted interior walls in off white (it's a bit dark inside) were facelessly offered a limited range of wallpapering or else! *The Shepherd*, as I said, is a tavern of rural antiquity, and nobody, customers or tenants, desired to be imprisoned in birch glades full of nubile nymphs being chased by *shaggy* shepherds, or candy-floss roses, or plushy 'flock', or jolly huntsmen chasing bushy-tailed foxes. But the jolly huntsmen they got, whether they liked them or not. Big Brother did, and that was that. They were the best of a bad lot.

Now, in the place of the old post-sign of a crook-holding old man in a smock with a lamb under one arm, there appeared an ominous rectangle swinging in its metal frame. 'TEMPORARY SIGN' declared this augury of questionable things to come. Without any preliminary warning of intent three impersonal persons just turned up one morning with extending lightweight ladder, bag of tools and 'TEMPORARY SIGN'. They moved into instant action.

'Hey, there', cried out the landlord, 'What the hell are you doing? Who are you, anyway?'

'Just carrying out orders, Guv', said the headman, 'Putting this up till the new one arrives.'

'In heaven's name, *what* new one?' demanded the tenant (whose rent was doubled without notice a year back), 'What's it going to be?'

'Search me, Guv. All we've been told to do is this.'

And they went right ahead and did it!

Visions spring to mind of dark-suited Metropolitan Men with butchy spectacles – or spider-thin gold-framed seeing aids – seated in some multi-storey block that is for never rural England. They are looking at colour charts, lettering and layouts displayed before them by a pushy young reject from the Slade.

'What we want, P.J., is an eye catcher'.

'Something, P.J., which will really catch the eye, you mean?'

'That's right, P.J. What we *don't* want is confusion. A village pub's called *The Dun Cow* — right?'

'Right. Well, let it be. But so far as we're concerned it's ours, and our *name* takes precedence over everything, and we want our *name* to be bold as brass – big, and bold as brass.'

'Brass, gentlemen,' says the display bloke, 'Is the very thing I have in mind. Bold, big and – er – brassy. But brassier than brass if you get my drift. Something like this.'

'Hm. Certainly smacks you in the eye, P. J. Brassier than brass. I rather like that.'

'I agree. Yes – I *like* it. Couldn't miss it on a winter night in Bootle.'

'And in one of our smaller properties out in the sticks – you'd certainly not miss seeing it there. And, mind you, P.J., just because they're small doesn't mean that they haven't got big potential – a future, I mean. And it's our business to put them just there – in the future. Why, I was told about one of ours down in Suffolk only the other day, sitting on the edge of planning permission for an Estate of three hundred bungalows right on its back doorstep.'

'P.J.' turns to the display merchant. 'Mr Gripping, what I like about your lettering is the way it stands out, as it were, from the background . . .'

'The *bas-relief*, you mean, sir?'

'Yes – the – er – *bar* relief, as I'd like to call it. Bar relief, eh? Perhaps there's a thought there. But, Mr Gripping, hand painting the effect might be a shade costly – no?'

'*Hand*-painting, sir? Oh, I wasn't thinking of anything like that, sir. Plastic moulding was what I had in mind. There you'd have the real thing with the lettering *really* sticking, as it were – out. Cut your costing by a good seventy per cent, I'd say, and I know just the people. . .'

Imaginary conversation? Of course, but what other type than this one wondered could produce the unimaginative heavy plastic hand affronting the simple occupants and gentle clientele of such one-time rural beatitudes as *The Ancient Shepherd*?

The mind returns to a mere decade ago when a faceless someone in the brewing hierarchy seemingly came by an abundance of copper far too good to miss at the cut-rate for bulk. Copper, eh? *Copper!* But, of course, a new, glowing and warmhearted image for every rural tavern under the batswing of Big Brother Brewery. Copper topped bars, so that every customer would know just where he was, and every landlord's wife know where *she* was after breakfast every morning striving to up-bright her copper tops from the previous day's overspill of beer and butts.

Out with all the patina of ancient oak and mahogany, and in with the new country-trend 'thing'. Copper. Old Ned Noakes, game-keeper retired, immaculate octogenarian in cord breeches, leather leggings and shoes daily hand polished to shine like old chestnuts, took his first look at the new-burnished copper bar top at *The Bay Horse* in Gosling Green, and said: 'I never see the like afore, not in a pub, that is. But they do say that on domes and Church roofs that it turns a decent sort of a green. A pint of the usual, missis, and I hope I lives to see the day, that's all.'

And so said all of us, and so we'll say again concerning the new signboard of *The Shepherd* in egg yolk and 'bar relief' white lettering. We hope we'll live to see the day when our rude north-easterlies, midsummer suns and equinoctial gales have blown and burned the plastic proclamation into tat and tatters. But knowing Big Brother Brewer, he has probably pinned upon us an image plastically, fibrously indestructible. The dear old *Shepherd* may go up in flames, but the other thing will lie bright and pristine on top of the pyre.

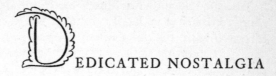

CHAPTER FIVE

DEDICATED NOSTALGIA

DURING A CERTAIN Energy Crisis 'The General', who lives in a village some three miles over the hills from our Parish Pump, thought he'd better take a look at his bicycle which for many, many years had stood motionless behind a pile of tea chests at the back of his small weather-boarded barn. An excellent repository for The General's Mini, the old barn, as well as for practical gardening equipment, hand-mower, rakes, hoes, spades, shears, mouldering wooden wheelbarrow, a pair of rotting beehives, flower pots and other items suitable for an old soldier's retirement. Also, it appeared, for tea chests containing relics of The General's distinguished and lengthy service in faraway outposts of the one-time Empire.

'Must get down to going through those tea chests of mine one of these days', 'The General' would frequently observe, 'The Lord knows what I might find in 'em. That's if the mice have left anything. Amazing what you collect after a long time in the Service. Yes, I'll get down to them one of these days. . .'

What he did get down to in a patriotic gesture in the face of the emergency, was the bicycle. Rims and spokes were rusted, unlubricated chain rigid with age, saddle mildewed, bicycle bell with its dome missing and bicycle basket tattered after long occupancy by mice. Tyres flat and perished.

'Got my old boneshaker out the other day', said The General, who rather shamefacedly had travelled on one of his fairly frequent visits to *The Star and Wheelbarrow* by Mini, 'Looks to me as though the old girl's due for the Last Post. Hrrrmph.'

'The General' is one of the few human beings known to me who really do contrive to partner lungs, larynx, palate and nose to produce that comment on the passing moment which can only be written down as 'Hrrrmph'.

Yes, the 'old girl' was surely ready for the Last Post, but the energy crisis had so loudly sounded the Reveille that none was surprised when the old gentleman came panting through the village in partnership with a 'new girl', a two-wheeled lady shining bright with chrome and body-worked in somewhat psychedelic green.

'Not exactly my style', proclaimed The General, 'but it seems that they don't turn out the kind of thing which I need in black any more. So I had to settle for this contraption. I very well dare say it won't look too bad once the shine's worn off a bit.'

He had, he said, well earned his pint that morning, saved the cost of a couple of quarts of the other stuff, 'done his bit' for the nation and made a sound investment into the bargain. 'Daresay I'll feel a bit stiff in the morning', added The General, making his way pint in hand and fistful of tokens in the other towards the gaming machine which stands in a far corner of '*The Star*' under the name 'Wheel of Fortune'.

A dedicated addict of the fruit machine is this old soldier, but well disciplined to confine his stakes to an average of 10p, sometimes when in the mood to 20p. Should turnover result in a hundred per cent profit, then this is firmly pocketed against the following day's flutter. Sometimes: 'By Gad! I've got the damned thing up', will be the cry against the merry tinkle of a torrent of tokens, 'Pint for me and a packet of filthy filters for the Memsahib.'

It was a happy reward for the patriotic gesture of the psychedelic bicycle that the Jackpot came pouring forth at the third pull of the first day. 'Good for you, General', came the truly meant cry of the three ancient men assembled.

'Calls, I think, for pints all round, gentlemen'. But The General was quick to make it clear that this created no sort of precedent. But it *was* a special sort of day, with lapwings seen from saddleback as never seen before, feasting goldfinches in view over hedgetops and the wind on the heath, brother, whispering through the spokes of crisis-conscious transport. Good for The General!

'Rather reminds me of the time when we were stationed at Chukkahabad – borrowed the R.S.M's bicycle just for the fun of it and rode ten miles to the nearest village – place called Slota, or Slahta, or some such name. The things I saw that I'd never noticed before, down in the wadis, you know . . . '

'Reminds me of when I was in. . .' A great 'When-I-Wasser. . .' is The General. To those of us who *weren't* anywhere very far beyond Venice, and not for very long at that, the 'When-I-Wassers', especially old soldiers, tea planters, rubber planters, Colonial Administrators and such cattle proclaim their far-flung pasts with dedicated nostalgia. These are non-conversational terrains unknown to most of us who dwell around the Parish Pump. Tales of thieving houseboys, spiders big as kittens, monsoons, Persian markets, drunken junk crews about Hong Kong, punka-wallahs, rickshaws, Chinese shop keepers in Singapore, man-eating tigers and the licentious debaucheries of 'other ranks'.

The only other 'When-I-Wasser' in the village is old Joseph Crane, bachelor rising ninety, who lives out his days in a large wooden vehicle which once did duty as sleeping quarters for the steam traction crews which travelled from farm to farm in threshing season and lived on the job.

Joseph, before he was invalided out of the Service, served three years in India as one of the cookhouse brigade. 'Joseph over there will know what I'm talking about', says The General from time to time, as he describes the invasion of his quarters by a king cobra.

Joseph does *not* know what 'The General' is talking about, since the great sub-continent seemingly made little impression upon him. He didn't think a lot to it is about as far as Joseph will go. He does not remember precisely where he was at any one time during those three years. There were, he recalls, great numbers of untrustworthy brown-skinned subhumans all over the place. 'Do you in the eye soon as look at ye' is Joseph's over-all summing up and indictment of the entire population of India, from Maharajas and Brahmins down to Untouchables. Joseph does *not* know what The General is talking about – in general – but he once trumped the other's ace king cobra by saying: 'I'll tell ye what I did see when I was out there – a little old porcupine shoot one of his quills six foot, if it were an inch, at a river rat. *And* he missed it.'

'Oh, rubbish, Joseph, that old wives' tale about porcupines shooting their quills – absolute rubbish.'

'I tell ye, I seen it with me own eyes, and seeing's believing, isn't it?'

'No, no, Joseph, it just won't do.'

'King cobras won't do, either, come to that. I never did see one of they – leastways, not in *my* cookhouse.'

Joseph rammed home his pipe between his teeth, and that, so far as common ground in India was concerned, was that!

The March winds of change blow about the Parish Pump. Those who were school kids only yesterday, it seems, are now young-middle-aged men with Cuban-style moustaches and kids of their own. Old Mrs Barter, and two other human antiquities, fell foul of effort and life just before and just after the Festive Season and everybody said: 'Funny how it always seems to happen around Christmastime.' Old Mrs Barter kept her fat cat, Sooty, on the window sill in summertime and by the fire in winter. Sooty was never during the fourteen years of a lifetime allowed out of doors. 'She might be a naughty girl if I let her out' Mrs Barter would explain, 'She's better off inside with me, cats being what they are.'

Men being what they were, old Pete Barter was never allowed *indoors* of a night time, but, his wife explained, was better off with his paraffin stove and camp bed in the out-house. After his 'sad loss' old Pete let the cat into the great outdoors where it liked it not and it died. Pete went within to cosy up beside the kitchener, likes it very much and lives.

As for Ethel Barter, it is to be hoped that she has travelled to some genial beyond untroubled by she-cats and he-men – such creatures being what they are.

CHAPTER SIX

No CHANGE OF THRUSH

I AM ALMOST hypnotically addicted to the morning rally, just outside my cottage door, of the 'school-lift mums'. These ladies, generally in the neat trim of slacks and sweaters, are a company of very cool cookies indeed, as they rendezvous in their Mini-Travellers and suchlike to deliver their chattering bratlings to whichever 'mum' or 'mums' is, or are, doing morning rota duty for the particular day.

They pack in the kids as though they were bottling plums. 'Now, come along, Samantha, into the back with you with David and Terry and Susan. Peter and Marybell in the front with me, and slam that door properly, Peter. And you'll bring my lot back with you this afternoon will you, Miriam? Right – that's it. Ye-es, you can sing your song, Susan. . .'

The 'delivery' mums stand for a while by the brookside, verbally machine-gunning one another about only-the-mums-know-what. Then with terminal rifle-shots of 'Bye, now', into their vehicles they step. Starters bark like dogs, engines rev up, wheels scatter the gravel of the brookside lane, and away they go, winkers winking, to their several destinations.

Within moments of their departure Mr Jasper Pettigrew, road-man retired of this Parish, emerges from his own cottage door, carrier bag in hand, and starts footing it with leisurely pace towards the village shop, half a mile up the road. Mr Pettigrew believes in getting in first before the womenfolk crowd the place out, like – Mr Pettigrew says – 'a jabber of little starlings'. His timing enables him to arrive at the garden gate of his 'little old mate', Tom Dixie, and spend a statutory ten minutes' interchange of news and views. At one minute past nine o'clock shop-opening Mr Pettigrew is eyeing the shelves.

Mr Pettigrew, whom I would never dare address as Jasper, is a figure of Patrician bearing, with a Romanesque profile and silver-grey wolfish curls at the nape of his neck beneath the chequered tweed cap. He looks like a turn of the century Liberal statesman, and always did, even while, as a roadman, minding his margins. He is somewhat of a dandy, and, upon certain summer Sundays, wears what must be among the last pairs of black-striped white flannel trousers in the United Kingdom. A sun-bitten straw hat replaces the tweed cap, and on the feet is a pair of those white buckskin shoes with leather garnishing, once known as 'Co-respondent shoes'.

School-lift mums, Jasper Pettigrew, Dixie-at-the-gate, brewers' dray prompt at 11.30 Fridays outside *The Star and Wheelbarrow*, the 11.15 a.m. appearance over the field path of 'The General' in Norfolk jacket, knickerbockers and deerstalker 'walking' his very old golden retriever which looks – like the General's hat – as though the moths had been busy in the fabric. Sometimes the old soldier comes by Mini. General and dog enter *The Star* for a beer and a biscuit at 11.30 precisely – except on Fridays when the draymen with ropes, pulleys and bottles in metal containers tear the tavern apart with their shouting and their shindy.

Thus the almost unalterable punctuation of the weekday days about the Parish Pump. There is something easeful and comforting about these human conformities to habit. 11.15 without the General would seem like Poachers' Wood without the seasonal windflowers, the elms of March unracked by rooks, the month of April untrumpeted by daffodils and without a swallow in the sky between the twelfth and the twentieth day.

It is great easement to the mind when its bearer, returning from the capital, or from farther-flung and longer absences, beholds the dark robes of the Vicar fluttering batlike at the South Porch of the Church. Ah! the Vicar *en route* for Vespers. It must be – and it is – exactly 6.25. One can set one's watch by the Vicar, as by the flat-capped spindleshanked figure of the Manor House gardener wobbling from the driveway on his rusty bicycle, homing for dinner. We don't need the voice of William Hardcastle on the car radio to tell us that this is 'The World at One'. George Merrick on his bicycle does it for those of us who chance to pass him on passage under the chestnut trees within the territory which surrounds the Parish Pump.

City visitors, weekending, say sometimes: 'You're becoming a cabbage, that's what. It's this "knowing where you are" which would drive me mad.' Into *The Star and Wheelbarrow* at five minutes past one precisely comes the squat figure of Ben Grudging. His pint stands ready poured for him. Only a stranger unknowingly at rest in Ben's corner of the settle would not move away from this place of long-seated right of occupation. At around one thirty it is traditional for somebody to say: 'Got the right time, Ben?' The fat old gun-metal 'turnip' watch is hauled from the waistcoat pocket at the end of its albert chain. 'Foive 'n twenty parst', says Ben. His little old watch is always spot on, but all the world knows that it is set to the second by the one o'clock pips. None who know him would dream of depriving Ben of this timely cushion of importance. He just *is* the authority of G.M.T. 'Never lorst or gone on a minute in fifty years' says Ben of the old gun-metal 'turnip'. Pure bunkum, we know, but this homely punctuation of the day must be forever honoured. It is Ben's watch which sends the regulars heading for 1.30 dinnertime, and this makes Ben feel good as God!

Ting-tang-ting-tang-ting-tang sounds the motor-horn bell by the crossroads where the big willow hangs its tresses out upon the wind. Ting-tang-ting-tang. We know not only that it is 1900 hours, give or take five minutes, but that it is Thursday – should we have forgotten. It is Webster's Fish and Chips upon its rustic round, regular in its piscatorial providence of an evening as is the 6.30 a.m. wakey-wakey of the gravel-laden heavy vehicle which rackets through the village every weekday morning to remind us that our own workaday time is right ahead.

Silence, then, growingly punctuated by small familiar sounds of consoling and containing comfort, and then the quick, nervy rhythm of commuter cars timing the 8.10 to the last second, followed by the steady footsteps of Miss Parkinson and her friend, Elizabeth, breeders of labrador bow-wows, passing towards the chalk ridge with hounds straining at leash. Up there, upon the thin and breezy downland, the dogs run free. With the wind in the east we hear the thin whistling of the ladies summoning the pack to heel, to leash for the road walk back to kennels. After 8.45 Miss

28

Parkinson and her friend Elizabeth are never seen again by anyone. Where do they shop, where if anywhere do they go? We know only that the dogs must be O.K. by the midday chuntering, Mondays and Fridays, of the Dog Food Van, down the street and up the short lane where ladies and labradors have their being.

We do not need the calendar or the air of dis-ease about the village to tell us that, once more, it is Good Friday. For here he comes again, as every year upon this day, the old man in the red woolly hat and breeches, upon his tricycle, eyes steadfast upon the road, saddle bag behind him. Another year has passed in the whisper of his spokes and narrow tyres, freewheeling down the churchyard hill. Whence, and to where, and why, forever, does he honour us in his passing upon that sad Friday which men call 'good'? Doubtless some other Parish Pump than ours knows that, by the tricyclist's passing, it is Whitsuntide – Spring Holiday. And upon late August's Summer Holiday most surely folk staring from the benches outside some other *Star and Wheelbarrow* – in Somerset, Warwickshire, Suffolk, who knows? – will say: 'Ah, here he comes again. Last holiday before Christmas.'

And will he pass us by this Eastertide as ever is? If he does not, then surely we must assume that it is for him that the bell has tolled and that Good Friday, sad day, will be the sadder for his absence, the old tricyclist of the red and woolly hat.

The comforting unadventurous punctuations of the Parish, a microcosm of a world set in its ways. And why not? How cogently such attitudes were expressed by H. H. Munro ('Saki') that enamelled miniaturist in the field of suave satire. We remember how Clovis, *enfant terrible* of non-conformity, attempts to inject a spurt of *vive la différence* into the stick-in-the-mud routine of an ancient brother and sister.

'Now take that thrush singing out there' says Clovis – or words to that effect – 'Think what a delightful surprise it would be if one day there was some different bird singing and the thrush was nesting somewhere else. . .'

'Oh, I scarcely think', says brother to sister, 'that at our time of life we would much care for a change of thrush.'

The unforgettable, unforgotten last word on the subject!

CHAPTER SEVEN

COTTAGE LOAF AND CAULIFLOWER

SUDDENLY, IF NOT wholly unexpectedly, the blow has fallen, for there, rising from her kitchen floor from her plump little knees and facing the mistress of the house, tears in her big brown eyes, stands Mariegold.

'Why, Mariegold, whatever's the matter. Is something wrong?'

There has, we well know, been something not wholly *right* about Mariegold these several months past. She has been wheezing rather, and not looking quite the same fresh-baked little cottage loaf who has brightened our lives, cleaned the silver, brought a rich patina to the furniture and hands-and-kneesed the kitchen floor for over twenty years of Tuesday mornings. She has spoken about her back, and a cold she don't seem to have been able to get rid of. Something of the familiar jolly lustre has been rubbing off our Mariegold for quite a while, and now comes the stunning truth of the matter.

'Oh, Mrs Grey, madam, I don't rightly know how to say it. But – but, I shan't be coming to you no more, not after next Tuesday. The Doctor says I've not got to go out to work no more – least-ways, not more than one morning a week.'

It is to be life without Mariegold. Oh God, Oh Montreal!

'Oh – *Mariegold* – oh, I *am* sorry. Now let's sit down and have a cup of tea and you can tell me all about it.' Tears brim in the eyes of the mistress of the house now, and they pour in cataracts down Mariegold's fat little old face. 'There, there, Mariegold, don't cry.'

Mariegold, it seems, has had to go into hospital twice for X-rays. Her chest, and her back. 'Of course, Mrs Grey, madam, he's put

31

me on tablets, but they don't seem to do no good, and now – and last night in surgery he said this.'

'Oh, Mariegold, I *am* sorry.'

'He says I've got to stop going to all my ladies. I said I couldn't quite rightly not go to old Mrs Parker and tidy her up once a week, and he said well, he said just the one, Mrs Upson, he said, but for your own good – and Mr Upson's – he said, you've just got to take it easy. I've been doing too much, he said. Oh, Mrs Grey, madam, and after all these years. Whatever'll she do without me? I said to the Doctor, and all he said was that you'd have to find somebody else and that was that.'

It is only right and proper that if it is to be 'only one morning a week' old Mrs Parker with her own eighty odd years and pair of bad legs should take priority over the other three of us for whom Mariegold has 'done' over the years. We think, mind you, that Mariegold likes us the best of all, and certainly more than poor old Mrs Parker who, according to Mariegold, 'does go on at me sometimes.' We know that she thinks young Angela Blenkiron of Barley Mill too bossy and 'hoity-toity', and that she is unhappy with bohemian and slap-happy Pat Saunders. 'You can't get on with your work down her place for the cats. Not that Miss Saunders isn't a nice enough person, but it's them cats – bits of fish and lights and that everywhere. But she's nice enough in herself if you know what I mean, Mrs Grey, madam.'

But we know where Mariegold's loyalty and love lie. She has watched our children grow into man's and woman's estate, and has christian-named them from near infancy, though it's always been 'Mrs Grey, madam', and 'Mr Grey, sir' to us. Mariegold knows all our funny little ways, and we know hers, some of them maddening such as the blind eye she turns, for some inscrutable reason, to the Sheffield Plate wine coasters, her habit of doing the floor of the downstairs loo but refusing to touch the wash hand basin, and her unfinished song which comes and goes between the howls of the Hoover. It's about some 'long time ago when there came a beggar in the snow, singing of the holly and the goose on the green. . . ' 'I learned it at school, and I don't never seem to be able to get it out of my head, Mrs Grey, Madam.'

Funny little things like that: like her positioning of every item upon the overmantel in the order in which *she* thinks they should be, her placing of jugs, decanters and so on with their handles left-handed, not right-handed, the Mariegold touch with the bathroom which finds my hair brushes reproachfully washed and laid straight every fourth Tuesday and my razor placed on the shelf furthest *away* from the hand basin. Always, with 'Mrs Grey, madam', the eleven o'clock break for a cuppa, and the news from all corners of the Parish – news of cats run over, the goings-on at the Youth Club Wednesday, parishioners dramatically 'fetched away' to hospital, certain maidens who ought to get married before they has to, the lady who 'did go on' about her holiday in Turkey or some such foreign place at the W.I. last week. And have we heard that the Rudds are leaving, that a deer got into the allotments Thursday and ate up half the spring greens, that Alf Dodmore's 'bronicals' goes from bad to worse.

Dear old Mariegold with her annual Christmas present to 'Mr Grey, sir' of five small cigars, and to 'Mrs Grey, madam' of bath crystals: her steadfast conviction that I, 'Mr Grey, sir', ought to go to London Tuesdays and not other days, so that Mariegold may give that study of mine a real, proper old clean-up, for you never saw such a mess. Over my dead body, Mariegold, dear. Poor old Mariegold, Queen of polishers, boss of her system with which we have never interfered, supper-up of cuppas, ending the morning three hour stint dead on the dot of twelve thirty on the furthest north-westerly kitchen tile. Now put out to grass like some old working farm horse got a bit past it.

'Oh, Mrs Grey, madam, and after all these years. Whatever'll you do without me?'

And how, we wonder, are the other two bereft ladies of the Parish going to get along without Mariegold? Miss Pat Saunders pinning a notice to the Post Office board: 'Daily Help Wanted, Thursday mornings only'. Young Mrs Angela Blenkiron hoity-toitily outraged at being let down without notice, and where was *she* going to 'get another woman'? Ah, where, indeed, because the Parish Mariegolds are scarce as snowballs in the Sahara. All, all are bespoke, but we wouldn't put it past Angela Blenkiron to get her unscrupulous little paws under the counter somewhere and collar stringy old Mavis – hard worker – from one or other of the households which depend upon her. Time will show.

'So we've lost our Mariegold – isn't it *too* ghastly for words?'

Yes, yes, Angela, it is indeed, but I'm not telling you yet what *we've* got—ha-ha! You'll find out. The word will get around. Thanks to cool thinking, quick thinking, realistic action and dropping the right word in the right quarters, *we've* got Susan Bilberry from Gosling Green, that's what!

Close friends in Gosling Green. Look, we've lost our Mariegold. Do you by any chance know of anyone here? One morning. Collect and deliver. Your *Susan*? You'll ask her? You think she might be interested? Her Tuesday morning people have sold up and gone, have they, and Susan doesn't fancy the newcomers. At least, not the look of them. You feel sure she'd rather come to us, do you? That's if she fancies going anywhere. Well, bless you, and you'll ring, will you – after you've asked her if she might be interested?

Eureka, she *is*! And there before her cottage door stands Susan, wiping pudgy hands upon the apron which covers an old woollen dress. If Mariegold was like a jolly little cottage loaf, Susan wears the homely crinkles of an almost fresh cauliflower. She is nervous. So are we. Won't we come inside, and forgive the mess. Mess? There is no mess. Susan's kitchen is as bright as that old new pin, her parlour smelling of lavender polish, her potted plants exuberant with bloom, her cat fat on the mat. Well, could she, would she, might she, will she? She's talked it over with 'her Bert' (we'll hear all about Bert in time!), and yes, she'll come, if we'll collect her nine thirty next Tuesday.

We have had a fortnight 'doing without' Mariegold, and now we have a week to get the place looking nice for Susan. Heavens! What *will* she think of the place? The threadbare carpet under my knee-hole desk, the damp patch in the kitchen, the living-room curtains in their seventh year, my grubby eiderdown, my grubbier dressing-gown, the two chipped teacups (better hide those), the almost unbelievable confusion in 'Mrs Grey, madam's' glory hole upstairs.

The sewing machine, the typewriter on its ash-covered table, the piles of half-finished exercises in oil painting, the woollies hanging out to dry on the makeshift line over the night storage heater. The books, the clothes, the children's Teddy Bears – never throw away a Teddy Bear – the old metal box of household files, all that is the heart of 'Mrs Grey, madam'. With what kind of a cold, clinical eye glinting from the cauliflower countenance is Susan going to make of *this* dump?

How hard we worked to wash the paint, polish the silver, call in the window cleaner, wash the bedspreads, fertilise the house

plants, block up the mouse holes, shampoo the carpets and generally treacle up the *ménage* as something fit for Susan to enter. Seldom
in Mariegold's time had such an exercise in self-respect been exer-
cised. We had always, lethargically, left it all to Mariegold, the one
who had known our ways for five-and-twenty years and 'did it
her way'.

There seemed, at the end of the week, little reason for Susan to
come at all, and, when inevitably she did, would we have enough of
the right kind of floor polish, furniture polish, brass polish and
silver polish to suit Susan? Unaffordable new wallpaper, new
vacuum cleaner, new dustpan, brooms and brushes mounted like
thunderclouds in the sky.

'Well, Susan, here I am, spot on time, eh? Yes, it *is* a lovely day.
As you say, makes it feel good to be alive. Oh, dear, your Bert's
"on the Club" with his shoulder this week, is he? I *am* sorry. You
keeping well yourself? Good . . . Lived long in Gosling Green,
have yo? . . . Good gracious! *Really*. . .?'

'I'm afraid – I'm afraid – I'm afraid. . .' we say to Susan. She, casting
a cordial eye around, shows no trace of fear. She sizes up the plug
points, asks for 'Glow-Pol' which she always uses, likes tea, not
coffee, at eleven, says she'll do the windows once a month. Best of
all, she looks at 'Mrs Grey, madam's' glory-hole, the shame-room,
the family 'hold-all'. 'Oh!' says Susan, 'What a dear little room!
Looks really lived in, don't it? And them Teddy Bears. . .'

We think it's going to be O.K. with us and Susan around the
Parish Pump. But, Mariegold, Mariegold, we shall ever miss you
and that 'beggar in the snow, singing of the holly and the goose on
the green. . .' Sleep well, dear old Mariegold, in your taking-it-
easiness, and don't fret about 'strangers mucking the old place
around.'

Cauliflower Susan doesn't sing, but she doesn't half bang about!

CHAPTER EIGHT

Sweet Lovers Love the Spring

ONCE UPON A time there was a fair-sized pond back of the village green, decently railed around, presumably to halt headlong village kids in their tracks before they helter-skeltered into it; and also to warn stranger motorists coming round the blind bend that there was this watery hazard. Farm ducks dibbled and paddled in the pond, and snoozed on hot afternoons about its banksides. Our ducks, Frances and Drake, had plenty of time for the pond.

The Parish Pump stood nearby, and was much used in those far-off days before water came gushing from the mains. Morning and evening the pond and Parish Pump privided an easy ambience for gossip and greeting across the brimming pails. At the far side of the green stood the village school, a bizarre piece of late Victoriana. The designer obviously got the bit between his teeth with that school. Its walls were of red brick, but its window mullions were of stone, and emphatically 'Gothick'. To make sure that the structure didn't collapse, the builder attached stern stone buttresses. In each of the gable fronts were stone slits, suggesting that arrows might be shot from them. There were battlements from which any teacher, if besieged by her pupils, might pour pitch or boiling oil. To cap it all the 'architect' planted on top a pair of outsize Tudor barleysugar chimneys.

The pond was great ,and so was the school. Neither are there any more. The duck pond has been filled in to accommodate one end of an open Dutch barn. Where the school stood is part of the garden of what Mr Osbert Lancaster would call a 'pseudish' new residence, with gables in the slightly Netherlandish style. The garden is inoffensively hedged around with Lonicera. And, inevitably, there's a weeping willow in the centre of the front lawn.

The first faint flavour of suburbanisation is drifting around the Parish Pump. Without shame I believe that the old pump water tasted sweeter than the stuff which, odourised with fluoride, spurts from our taps. I believe that the pagan innocence of May Day as it used to be with the school upon the green, was more wholesome than watching Speakers' Corner on the telly.

Ah, me! May Day! Once upon those times before the village school was rubbed out there were children about the village all day and every day. They carolled at Christmas time, conkered in November, whipped tops at Eastertide and celebrated May Day with a fervour which they knew to be fun, but did not recognise as something most exuberantly pagan.

For many days beforehand there were dedicated deliberations in the schoolroom, pre-election campaigning followed by a going to the polls for the voting. Who would be Queen of the May this year, and who her decidedly substandard Consort, May King? Also, from the unseen playground back of the school would be heard wiry strains of music from Miss ('Teacher') Cribbidge's old portable gramophone.

May morning, in those high and far off times. seemed always to break with a windless radiance over a surf of blossom. From dawn the song birds chimed from horizon to horizon, and in an abundance and variety surely far greater than the choruses of today. If it were ever dull or rainy upon May morning, then I've forgotten it. The sun shone, the air over the brook was alive with swallows and martins, and I will swear that there was always dew laid on *in memoriam* to the milkmaids who had once dabbled in it.

At eight o'clock precisely the children assembled upon the green, the little girls draped in what seemed to be mum's muslin curtains and the boys rather sheepishly in nothing more than their Sunday best. Two chairs from the schoolroom were placed upon the green. In the one sat the elected May Queen, in the other her Consort. 'I hereby duly crown your Majesty as Queen of the May', piped last year's May Queen, placing upon the Royal brow a chaplet of celandine, stitchwort, violet – anything that might be going. The May King got a small circlet, and both were given sceptres of green willow.

And then the Royal Progress around the village, from cottage to cottage, house to house, May Queen, May King, attendants, and general commoners a respectful pace or two behind the Court. All carried nosegays of wildflowers, and before the open doorways and windows of the village the children sang. They saluted the Merry, Merry Month of May; they piped of Lovers and their Lasses, of the Oak and of the Ash; in their earnest little voices the birds did sing, hey-ding-a-ding-a-ding, and sweet lovers loved the spring.

Of course cash donations were expected, for ceremonies of such magnitude could not be mounted for nothing. The old ribbons for the Maypole, for instance, were faded and torn, and replacements could hardly be demanded of the Local Education Authority. Of course we gave gladly, for who could do otherwise as the poorest return for such flower-decked bounty of the spirit!

At two o'clock in the afternoon and in the centre of the green, King and Queen upon their thrones commanded that the ritual of the Maypole dance be carried out. There was the pole, there were the coloured ribbons, and there, with his old brown fiddle, was 'Snobby' Harris, Practical Boot and Shoe Maker. All the village gathered around. We sat, or lay, in the grass and enjoyed with relish the twining and intertwining of the coloured ribbons, the hop-skip-and-jump of the dancers, the inevitable entanglements, the anxious visage of Miss Cribbidge.

On the last year of all, because Local Authority were laying a water mains extension over the green, the Maypole was banished to the meadow behind the village shop. Perhaps in that meadow things were even more ambrosial, since the meadow was brassy with buttercups, and the air fumed with the astringent breath of them and with the wings of honey bees. The shoes of the dancers were gilded with pollen, and Titania and Oberon would have nothing on our Royal Pair in their greatest hour.

All that was yesterday. Today the village kids are swept away each morning by bus to the big modern primary school four communities away. There is no May-Singing any more, no capering in innocence around the ancient symbol of fertility – if that it be!

The Parish Pump itself, of course, remains, but no sweet water spurts from its nozzle. Like Church and Village Hall, the cast iron convolutions of its pillar remind us that we are, indeed, a Parish. And we have recently held, what's more, that hard core of Local Government and rural democracy, the Annual General Parish Meeting.

I suppose we are fortunate in having as Clerk to the Council, Sebastian Crick, a full-time Chartered Accountant who commutes daily to London. He is pale, crisp and efficient. In other days it was Nathan Grossett, smallholder of this Parish, who was – still is – rubicund, plump and earthy. Nathan's mills ground exceeding slow, but in those days so did everyone else's. Nathan, of course, could never have dealt with these changed times in which, clawing on to our remaining amenities, we fight tooth and nail through our Council to conserve them.

'If I may raise a point, Mr Chairman. . .?'

'Yes, of course Miss, er – Mrs, er. . .?'

'*Miss* Agnes Stoker, "Dovetails". . .'

'Yes, of course, Miss Stoker – of course, you moved into "Dovetails" last June, didn't you? Yes, Miss Stoker. . .?'

'I moved into the village last June, yes, Mr Chairman. I accepted my surroundings in good faith. What I did *not* bargain for, Mr Chairman – and I think my neighbour, Mr Greatorex, will bear me out – what I did *not* bargain for was blowflies during July and August, and *every* Tuesday the hullabaloo from Mr Bull's barn over the road. . .'

Blowflies? Hullabaloo? Mr Greatorex of 'Honeysuckles' adds: 'And the stench, Mr Chairman, when the wind is due west.'

We feel sorry for the occupants of these two cottages with blowflies and stench from the new broiler houses to the west of them, and for the Tuesday practice in the barn over the road of our swinging Group, 'The Slipstream'. Since planning permission has been granted both by the R.D.C. and the County for the broiler houses there's not much that the Parish Council can do.

Farmer Grudging – broiler houses – flatly denies the hatching of blowflies within his hygienic chicken factory. An occasional slight effluvium? Possibly. But the countryside, he points out, is the countryside, and ripe rustic reeks are to be expected. Manure is manure is manure.

Sebastian Crick's Annual Report has covered a multiplex of issues – the churning up of the green by two Meets of the local Hunt: the pending action by the R.D.C. to restrain the car-breaker on the Muttering Road from further desecrating the landscape with rusty junk; a resounding defeat for a small Parish minority anxious for kerbed pavements and street lighting – 'We are not, ladies and gentlemen, a garden suburb.'

An angry voice: 'YET'.

The Clerk, the Chairman and the Council confess to possessing no powers to forbid the door-to-door activities of Jehovah's Witnesses, and have received the sympathetic, but firm, refusal of the Local Education Authority to allow fee-paying children at private schools to hop on to Comprehensive School buses. Fee-paying mums will just have to share out their kiddy-carrying as usual.

'If I, on behalf of my neighbours, were to put in my annual plea, Mr Chairman. . .?'

It is the unfortunate Samuel Brickett who, with his neighbours the Hemps and the Partridges, lives down in the mossy hole known as Watchitt Green. The by-way which leads to these three cottages and nowhere else is 'unadopted'. The Rural District Council wishes to know nothing of it. Winterlong the three households flounder in and out of their homes along an avenue of mud and cinders. Two years ago the neighbours clubbed together and bought a load of heavy gravel with which to fill up the pot holes.

'Yes, Mr Brickett, we'll certainly put your case to the Local Authority again – I scarcely feel with more potency than you and Mr Hemp and Mr Partridge have put it yourselves.'

'It's a disgrace', shouts Brickett, 'They should be forced to adopt it.'

Sebastian Crick rather smoothly suggests that since the three households have themselves taken care of the approaches, then the Council may well take the view that the by-way *has* been adopted – as a Private Road. And it is for ever more the responsibility of the 'adopters' to maintain it.

'Whose side are you on?' bawls Brickett.

'We are not here, Mr Brickett, to take sides', says Crick, very crisply this time, 'Only to take note of parishioners' interests and guard their amenities.'

'Our road *is* a bloody amenity, isn't it?' yells Brickett, 'We've got to *bribe* the coalman to come down. It's all very well for the rest of you . . .'

As always, on the annual occasion of the Parish Meeting, we are dumbfounded by the small multitude of unknown faces. They can't *all* be newcomers. Where do the half of them live? We do, at least now know, where Miss Agnes Stoker lives – in the cottage called 'Dovetails', bedevilled by blowflies in high summer, and deafened every Tuesday by the cacophony of 'The Slipstream'.

We shall probably not set eyes upon her for another year. Nor upon a great many other citizens who are our invisible neighbours in this rural community which straggles north, south, east and west of the Parish Pump.

CHAPTER NINE

UGGERNAUT

THE SHADES OF night were falling fast around the Parish Pump when the windows of *The Star and Wheelbarrow* were abruptly darkened by the wheeled cliff of the largest juggernaut vehicle ever seen by even the youngest inhabitant. The 'strange device' which it wore upon its side was not 'Excelsior', but some very unknown foreign words ending with the recognisable romantic city name of Buda-Pesth.

Buda-Pesth, eh? How and why had this evocation of the mighty Danube come to rest by the prattling waters of our chalky little English brook? Oh, yes, we all knew that we were 'in Europe', but surely not in this far, faraway Eastern part of the Continent. Hungary, with its gypsies, czardas and things, was nothing to do with the Common Market, was it? Yet there the monster stood outside our little pub far from any main highway and only connected with such by a spider-web of wandering byroads.

The door of the tap-room opened and in came the driver to be greeted by the appropriate hush which ever falls upon such occasions. He was a squat, swarthy and muscular young fellow wearing a woolly hat with a pompom and a smile to go with it. He carried a piece of paper on which was written with a felt pen the name of a village which was very very similar to that of our own. Indeed, that name spoken with a Hungarian accent could very well be interpreted as standing for *our* fistful of rural acres about the Parish Pump.

'Is please this place?', or a sentence to that effect, enquired the man from Buda-Pesth. He read aloud from his piece of paper without displaying it. It sounded *very* like our patch.

'Yes', said a customer, 'That's right, mate.'

'Is right – mate? Is what "mate"?'

'I mean, mate, as you're right where you thinks you are.'

'I am then here?' again asked the man from the banks of the distant Danube, and he stared at his piece of paper. Approaching the bar counter and planting a fifty pence piece thereon he pronounced the monosyllable unmistakable in any language of the world.

'Beer', said he.

Our landlord was quick to appreciate the complexity of saying something like: 'Yes, sir. What sort of beer? Straight Bitter, Keg or Draught Lager? Or we have Ploughman Strong, Light Ale, Brown Ale, Old Farmer, Dublin Black, Newcastle Brown, Mackintyre Export and I.P.A?' Without hesitation he pulled a straight pint of Bitter and set it before the visitor complete with change from fifty pence.

'Beer', said our landlord.

'Is good', proclaimed the European customer, adding: 'Beer – good!'

He drank deeply from his glass, smacked his lips, re-studied his piece of paper, fixed our landlord with a brown Hungarian stare, and said: 'I am here. Where is, please, the tractor factory?'

'*Tractor* factory? *Here*? We don't make tractors here, sir. Look, let's have a look at that piece of paper.'

All was made clear on the instant. The felt-penned name was that of a well-known area in the industrial Midlands, full fifty miles from our little hollow in the low East Anglian hills. From Harwich or Ipswich our man from Buda-Pesth had driven his juggernaut, map reading no doubt, and then, as he drew closer to the Parish Pump seeking direction by word of mouth. And here he was.

'Is no tractor factory here? Where is, please, the tractor factory?'

It all made quite a stirabout in *The Star and Wheelbarrow* that evening. How in hell to direct our Hungarian through dark and winding lanes to a recognisable motorway leading to what *sounded* like 'our place' somewhere south of Solihull? And where was the poor chap going to sleep?

No trouble there. After another couple of 'Beer – good's' we were led out to inspect the driving cab of the juggernaut. Folding bed, H and C, Campa-Gaz, locker full of canned goodies, radio, coffee pot.

44

'I put him somewhere on grass before tractor factory'.

We wished our bizarre visitor well as we saw his colossal cliff, tail-lights blazing, take the *wrong* narrow lane past the Parish Pump *en route* for the tractor factory.

Maybe, having found 'somewhere on grass', he'd be back in the morning. But we never saw the man from Buda-Pesth again!

What we do begin to see again and again as spring turns to summer, are the friends from the Metropolis. And most welcome they are, hard on the heels of the Friday night telephone – 'As it's *such* gorgeous weather we thought we'd take a little run out tomorrow . . . will you be at home? . . . no, *no* don't do anything special. . . we'll bring our own lunch and a bottle of plonk. . . it would be lovely to see you after all these months . . .'

Madge and Peter in their new Volvo, Susan and Tom in their old Mini, the 'fair weather friends' as we call them in jesting good nature. They sniff the lovely grass and stretch themselves upon it like sunlight cats. They gaze into the green corridors of the sycamore tree, wander down the brookside, watch the house martins rebuilding their home under the eaves of *The Star and Wheelbarrow* and stare across the rims of their pints at the ancient men of the village who stare back in a numbly accepting kind of way.

'Oh! but how lucky you are', they exclaim, 'to live in such an absolutely beautiful village! How we envy you!'

At that very moment a 'mystery tour' coach pulls up outside and forty or more matrons in hats and a handful of rather beaten-looking old men pour into tavern, a number of the ladies seeking out the 'Ladies' and the elderly men ordering up beers, sherries and shandys. Oh, it's all quite in order. They've been catered for. *The Star* expects them, and soon the sandwiches crowned with slips of cucumber arrive. Vagrant coaches are not made welcome, but this sort of thing is all part of the pattern of living in a beautiful village during the spring and summer months.

It can be both a privilege and a pain to live in a village of reasonably renowned charm, as is ours about our Parish Pump. We have to take the rough with the smooth, and the rough social side of it is when the cornfields ripen about our horizons, the flowering candles of bloom are alight about our casual chestnut trees, the swifts scythe the skies and the lanesides are surfed with cow parsley, hemlock, meadowsweet, wild carrot and yarrow. In fact – spring and summer. Few come to take pictures of us in dark wintertime. But in the sweet summertime – oh! brother!

It is flattering to be visited by camera clubs, and the countryside is an amenity rightfully accessible to all. But – 'Can I help you in any way?' I once had occasion to ask of a young man slung around with filters and lenses who was standing in the middle of my lawn squinting through a view finder at the back of the cottage. 'Yes', he said, 'If you wouldn't mind *just* for a second stepping out of the picture. Forgive the intrusion', he added, 'but I couldn't resist it, and I didn't think there was anybody at home. Lovely little place you've got here.'

'Glad you like it', was all I could manage.

'Super', he said, 'If these come out I'll be delighted to send you a couple of prints.'

I will say this for him – he did.

Admittedly the triangle of greensward which lies, unfenced, some twenty feet from the front door is what is defined as 'manorial waste', and consequently free for all. But the family party with folding table and chairs, sandwiches, thermos flasks and transistor radio in full view and earshot of the front windows did not improve the landscape one summer's day. They had every right to be there, so it was in a mood of guilt mixed with irritation that I stepped forth to say, with what I hoped was cutting sarcasm: 'The music is delightful, but *do* you think you could turn it down a bit?'

Father, without even turning round, cut down the volume a fraction. He made no comment. Mother fixed me with an outraged glare. Surely, this implied, it was a free country, wasn't it? The kids stopped turning cartwheels and somersaults and stared open-mouthed at the spoil-sport stranger.

'We do happen to live here', I said, rather lamely.

'Nice to be some people', said Father.

Such, of course, are the exceptions who outrage the patterns of our villages – beautiful in summertime in general, and of ours about the Parish Pump in particular. We have no quarrel with the urban cyclists whose spokes spin peacefully through the village of a summer weekend. They sit in the sunshine munching their sandwiches and studying their large-scale maps. Many of them in their late middle years wearing shaggy breeches or baggy shorts look like old-style Fabians, and bestow an air of solemn, healthy rectitude upon our scene. Motoring 'mimsers' – middle-of-the-roaders – occasion us no harm as, with a very old Gran and an

46

obvious Uncle and Aunt in the back, they trundle by in wayward admiration of the *mise-en-scene* But the 'night rally' lads and lasses with their thunderstorm shindys and bedroom-blinding headlamps are a very different proposition. Two such merry lads, seated in an open sports car and carrying clipboards, stopped outside our cottage a couple of years back, stared at its oddly isolated position, went into conference together, scribbled on their boards and stared at my out-coming wife.

Said the driver: 'Just to let you know, madam', 'that we'll be giving this place as a clue for a checkpoint a fortnight on Saturday. "Home Far From Homes" – how about that, eh? No objections, I trust.'

They seemed startled when my wife replied: 'Yes – every objection I can think of.'

'Oh, don't be like that, madam. It's all just in aid of a bit of harmless fun. After all, you were young yourself once, weren't you?'

'That's as may be', she admitted, recalling with decent nostalgia the treasure hunts of her maidenhood in a rusty old Renault, 'but I'm damned if I'm young now. Have your Check-Point-Charlie somewhere else. If you *must* come, why not make it the Parish Pump?'

'Tha-at's a good idea – a ve-ery good idea indeed. Charles, I've got it – "You can't fill up at this pump". How's about that?'

We heard them all right, all right, for what seemed half the night. But aren't we lucky to live in such a beautiful village!

CHAPTER TEN

HARRY FOR ENGLAND

A VERY GREAT many years ago when the merry bright blood of youth was singing through veins and arteries uncluttered by antiquity an eccentric young architect named Guildford Holliday came to the Parish. With his plump and peachy wife named Pansy he dwelled for three years among us, and none who were in the village at the time will ever forget the young Hollidays and Guildford's passion for giving parties upon sundry named days of the year. He celebrated the days of St. George, St. Andrew (Pansy was a Scots girl, even with a name like that) and St. Valentine. Hardly had Guildford shouted 'Harry for England' upon October the 25th, Day of St. Crispin, than he was at it again upon the 31st, All Hallows' Eve, dishing out home made cider and bidding the small company take bites at apples strung from the main beam of the cottage.

May Day, Trafalgar Day, the mid-point of the Lenten Observance all called for a Party at the Hollidays'. Guildford Holliday anticipated 'Plant a Tree' year by five and thirty years. Privily and stealthily by night he dotted several areas of what is known as 'Manorial Waste' with sapling limes, silver birches, wych-elms and sycamores. Furthermore, without any sanction sought of the Parish Council, no single member of which would undertake the slaughter of a sapling well rooted and planted. Only God, it must have been felt, could make a tree, and who were they to interfere with this celestial craftsmanship aided by its handyman-on-earth, Guildford Holliday? Guildford's trees are now grown to full and fine estate, a credit to the village amenities and a memorial to a bizarre character long vanished, the Lord knows where, from the cottage hard by the Parish Pump.

Midsummer's Day, or the evening thereof, once aroused a fever in Guildford which could have been either Druidic or Little-Peopled. For the Revels Pansy became Titania and Guildford Oberon. As for the rest of us we were greeted, across a fat beaker of home made mead, as Pease-Blossom, Cobweb, Moth and Mustard-seed.

> Weaving spiders come not here;
> Hence, you long-legg'd spinners, hence!
> Beetles black, approach not near;
> Worm nor snail, do no offence. . .

Thus boomed Guildford, pressing an old seventy-eight of the Mendelssohn on the turntable of the ancient radiogram. Behind the Hollidays' cottage garden with its crab-apple tree and corner plot of ground-elder which Guildford deliberately let grow for the sake of its furry flowers there stretched – and still stretches – the five or more acres of Spratt's Meadow. Two working shire horses grazed its summer pastures in those days and it was glazed with buttercups in season. There were mushrooms in abundance come September and several rings where the green of the grass was darker, proclaiming the presence of the spores beneath. 'Mushrooms there maybe', proclaimed Guildford, mead down gullet, tongue in cheek, 'but if you tell me that's only because of the horses, you're wrong. Horses don't walk around dropping that good stuff in neat circles, do they? Oh, no, there's more to mushrooms than horse manure. They're magic, they're manna and they're in the gift of the fairies – oh yes, oh dear me yes! And that's why we're gathered here tonight – come on, drink up. We're going to tread the light fantastic around those rings in Spratt's Meadow tonight, just to let the little chaps know that we're duly grateful.'

'Guildford, you're potty.'

'Potty I may be, but don't tell me that there aren't fairies at the bottom of my garden – especially *tonight*.'

It was the mead, of course, coupled with a drop of gin, old dear, and Guildford's compulsive rhetoric that did, indeed, see the lot of us prancing hand in hand around those fairy rings on that Midsummer's Night of long long ago. A sly moon toplit the fragrant darkness, and the fat shire horses snorted as though they, like our wishful-thinking and rather tipsy selves, sensed the shaggy presence of God Pan not so very, very far away.

That was another world when there were fairies at the bottom of the Hollidays' garden. Now in front of it, crutched upon a driveway of weedless gravel and behind a boundary of white posts and chain link fencing, is something very different, that almost arrogant image and proclamation of status, a boat. Where Guildford's ground-elder once flowered is a double garage for his and her's. That's all right, all right, but somehow it's that fibreglass boat, gleaming blue and white, which takes the biscuit. The 'Commodore' as some have begun privily to call him, has every entitlement to his boat, forward-cabin and all. But - and no sour grapes here – this boat upon its crutches fifty miles from the open sea arouses feelings of uneasiness. 'I've made it', shouts the boat, 'her master's voice'. All moving westwards along the street towards the *Star and Wheelbarrow*, or even to Church, have to pass the boat. Eyes tend to turn away, and it's not the sort of thing about which one can throw the flippant remark to the 'Commodore'. Such as, 'Any more for the *Skylark*?', or 'Why don't you rename the house *Smugglers*?'

'I – er – see you've got a boat' was about the best one managed to do at first encounter with the 'Commodore' after status was proclaimed.

'Yes', he replied, blushing a bit under his weekend jaunty little straw hat in the Caribbean style, 'Yes, I'm afraid we have. *Quite* unaffordable and unjustified, but we said to ourselves, we said, if we don't do it now, we never will, so we did. Bank Manager not too chuffed about it, ha-ha.'

'No, I – er – suppose not. Ha-ha! Well, I must be getting along. Time to take the daily lady home.'

It was too. Susan Bilberry, the new daily lady from Gosling Green. In all her lifetime of fifty or more years Susan has never strayed far beyond the boundaries of Gosling Green and may be defined as a lady of limited vision and elbow grease *beyond* limit. A century back and Susan would, doubtless, have expressed surprise by way of 'Lawks-a-mussy-me'. As it was in this century when, suddenly, she beheld the boat from the passenger seat of our car, she managed: 'Whoi, Mr Grey, whatever's that thing doing there? It's a boat, in't it? Whoi, whatever's come over the place!'

What, indeed, we ask ourselves?

Gosling Green where Susan has her being, just a couple of miles over the hill, is rather where we were some five and thirty years ago when there were fairies at the bottom of the Hollidays' garden and not a fibreglass boat in the front of it.

Gosling Green, being a hamlet, has its complement – rather as on a boat – numbered not in people, but in souls. A hamlet of about one hundred and twenty five souls, that's Gosling Green. There are geese upon Gosling Green, a barber who 'works Saturdays' in a tarred shed and a thatched tavern called *The Bay Horse*. It has become my habit, after depositing Susan at her garden gate just before one o'clock on Wednesdays, to brave the grand old men of Gosling Green in the Public Bar of *The Bay Horse*.

The bitter beer I knew came from the same, the ever reliable little country brewery so many of whose distinguished pints I have relished over the years in *The Star and Wheelbarrow*. But I do not venture into *The Bay Horse* just for the beer, but to gaze with something approaching awe upon the four ancient men who are the hard core of the tavern at dinnertime. Ancient men new to me, and of an antiquity which makes those wiseacres of *The Star* seem quite sprightly youngsters.

To the grand old men of Gosling Green I am, of course, known both as a name and a passing figure of long rural standing in the neighbourhood. But the figure of me taking my earthy sacrament at their own High Altar was something quite different. The dauntingly abrupt fog of silence which greeted my first entry is gradually giving way to guarded acceptance.

'Morning, gentlemen', I now say upon entry, and 'Mornin' ' muffle the tones of the ancient men, as they stir uneasily about their dominoes. They're domino-besotted up at *The Bay Horse*. Greedily the pieces are gathered in by hands like hooks of old oak, and deftly the curdled old eyes assess the merit of each gathering. The players are now known to me as Dan, Sam, Peter and Tom.

A week back, and for some reason dominoes were out, and proclamation of antiquity was in, Dan, said Tom, was 'Ten year younger'n me, ain't yer, mate?' 'Eh?' said Dan. 'Ten year younger'n me, I said to the gentleman, ain't yer, mate?'

'Older yer mean', croaked Dan, 'If I gets through ter November oi'll be nointy, that's what oi'll be. Nointy. Fair old age, nointy.'

He relit his three-inch tobacco pipe. They all lived long, they agreed, on account of the real meat they was brought up on. Meat that *was* meat, and plenty of it. Trouble today was the bullocks was killed almost afore they'd stopped being calves loike. No meat on 'em. There was fat beasts, fully 'growded' beasts in them days, beasts of many hundredweight with plenty of meat on 'em.

They growled on through a gastronomic jungle of batter pudd'n, red gravy, drippin', spuds as was spuds, real spuds, something to get the teeth inter'.

Were things truly like that, I wondered, as thoughtfully I drove home to a macaroni cheese.

ᴛHE MOST GOOD NATURED OF MADNESS

THEY CALLED THEMSELVES 'The Slipstream', did Mike, and Pete, and Ron and Lilian. Mike trebled on sax, trumpet and clarinet. Pete was on the drums, and Ron was guitar, electric and straight up-and-down. Lilian, a busty Norfolk dumpling of a young lady, belted out the songs in the manner of an amiable clod-hopping Lulu. Every Tuesday evening was practice night for 'The Slip-stream' in the small, well-heated barn across the meadow, kindly made available to them at no charge by farmer Bull. 'Just so long as ye don't upset the cattle', farmer Bull had said, 'ye can get your-selves up on the staging where the cornsacks lays.'

And so 'The Slipstream' did every Tuesday evening between seven and ten. The wintering cattle started lowing a bit, but as the months rolled by were struck, according to Mike, into a kind of hypnotised silence. 'No, I can't say as they danced exactly, but they did shuffle about a bit. We all seemed to get along together after a while.' It was an economically sensible arrangement, less costly than hire of the Village Hall, and evocative of a generally amused tolerance around the Parish Pump. 'The Slipstream' pro-duced a heartfelt, rhythmical shindy, enjoyed themselves and harmed nobody. The night owls above the meadow added their own melodious woodwind to the ensemble. The Group had no high-faluting ambition, knowing full well their limitations. They existed in the harmony of their rock'n-rolling, or whatever it was, and were much in demand at Saturday evening caperings in village halls for miles around.

One visitor to the village, seeing 'The Slipstream' with tubby

Lilian in a miniskirt leaving *The Star and Wheelbarrow* en route for Tuesday rehearsal in the barn, had the effrontery to fancy them 'long-haired layabouts, probably on drugs.' We soon cut this brash stranger down to size, since, whatever we may have thought of their cacophony, we held our 'Slipstream' in good regard. Long-haired – agreed. Layabouts – certainly not. Mike is a keen young craftsman learning his trade with a cabinet maker: Pete is a 'bricky' earning fat money with a building firm: Ron is second keeper on a huge estate: Lilian is a dentist's receptionist. They wear – barring Lilian – bush shirts and tight pre-faded jeans. Lilian's gear some-times looks like the skin of an old goat. But they are all of them a bunch of highly endearing youngsters, and we don't care for pom-pous strangers deriding 'The Slipstream' we loved.

I say 'loved', because 'The Slipstream' as a group with their own wild style are no more. The Tuesday evening thumpings, moaning, squealing have ceased. Like the cattle, now at pasture, and the Beatles, each one now 'doing it my way', 'The Slipstream' has split. With, let it be said, the greatest concord and amity. Pete the 'bricky' is departing with his firm to the Midlands: Lilian is about to marry the nephew of her dentist, and Ron has decided to go 'Folk-and-Up-Country' with a rather classy Group of that nature in Steepleborough. Mike, sax, trumpet and clarinet put by is, temporarily at any rate, a rustic Othello, all occupation gone. He may, he says, join up with a mob at Gosling Green known as 'The Routiers', though he fancies himself a shade above their class.

'The Slipstream' staged a farewell 'happening' in the Village Hall, admission 25p, plus a bottle of something. Any profit after hire of Hall to go to the 'Over Sixties'. Large numbers of non-attenders stumped up 25p-plus out of sheer affection for the exuber-ant 'Slipstream', a mighty nice little lot of happy kids. From half a mile away on a prevailing wind we could hear the thundering heartbeats of the Village Hall, and the lusty squalling of buxom Lilian. An extremely good time was clearly had by all, though many customers at *The Star and Wheelbarrow* on the Saturday morning wore a greenish tinge. The loose change was sufficient to mount a 'Mystery Tour' for the 'Over Sixties'. 'Long-haired laya-bouts', indeed! There aren't many of these about our Parish Pump.

Now it is summertime, time of strangers, beguiling glimpses of Europe and the world even farther afield on the vacational prowl about the Parish. A party of six Japanese ladies and gentlemen so slung about with lenses, colour filters and tiny tape recorders as to seem walking emissaries of Okasaki Audio Electronics Incorporated. Broad, toothy smiles, bowings, gushing, pentatonic-sounding praise for everything in eyeshot and earshot. Snip-click-snip of cameras, waggling of mini-mikes in front of the ducks upon the brook. Notebooks and clipboards, libations of vodka in *The Star*, brown-eyed scrutiny of the darts board. A year or two back, and we had a visiting party of Russian educationists with the eye of their Commissar upon them as they were introduced to the principles of what one of our Saloon Bar regulars described as 'Push Rouble'. The Soviet citizens were great value until the Commissar decided that there had been enough of 'Push Rouble' coupled with 'Pull Pint'. In the twinkling of an eye the tumult and the shouting died, and the merry men and maidens from Moscow filed silently into the night.

By the I's, the D's, the S's, the NL's and the F's upon the rears of their vehicles we are able, before we venture conversation, to nationalise our visitors. Italians, Germans, Swedes, Dutch and French. There was no sign of any kind upon the rear of the very ordinary English car which had decanted the two couples from Pennsylvania into *The Star and Wheelbarrow*. They sought lunchtime sandwiches. And they sought conversation with the natives. I'll say they sought it!

It was the older man who opened the bowling. I beg his pardon – 'pitching'. Straight to the rural point he came with the question extraordinary.

'Do you have much bother with ground hogs around these parts?'

'Ground hogs? Er – do you mean pigs? We have pigs of course, but they don't run wild.'

'No, sir, I do *not* mean pigs. I mean ground hogs. Woodchucks we call them back home. They dig holes, and when they come out of their holes they sit up on their hind legs and look around. The farmer's worst friend, I guess. Don't you get trouble with woodchucks around here?'

An old jingle remembered from childhood came to mind, and I let fly with it. 'How much wood would a woodchuck chuck if a woodchuck could chuck wood?'

'That's right, sir, that's surely right. I was taught that when I was a kid – no kidding. So you have them?'

'Well, no, actually we don't.'

'Chipmunks? Racoons? Swell pets, racoons. You don't have racoons?'

'No, no racoons.'

'Oh, but they're real cute, racoons', cried the younger of the two ladies, 'And you don't have any?'

'No, nor chipmunks, either. We've got foxes, badgers, water rats and – er, er – field mice.'

'Deer? Do you have deer around these parts?'

We were able to say that we did have a small herd living in an area of woodland nearby. Yes, they did get around. No, we didn't hunt them. That was to say – hrrrm – unofficially shoot them. This was not to say that the deer were *not* shot – strictly off the record.

'We certainly have to hunt ours', said the younger man.

'But I can tell you, sir,' said the older, 'the best shooting practice of all is to go after ground hogs. If a guy can get a ground hog at a hundred and fifty yards, then he'll have no difficulty in getting a deer at four hundred. I guess you don't get skunks over here?'

'A skunk', said the elder of the ladies, 'makes another swell pet. No, sir, I know what you're going to say, but catch a young skunk and give him the right operation, and you'll have no smell of skunk around the house. But ground hogs, nobody could want to make a pet of a ground hog.'

Suddenly, midfield of this lunchtime meeting bristling with question, answer and laughter, inspiration came. 'What we do have', I crowed, 'is not ground hogs, but hedgehogs. Do you have hedgehogs in Pennsylvania?'

Hedgehogs? *Hedge*hogs? 'Now what, sir, might a hedgehog be? Some kind of a wild pig, is it?'

'No, sir, it is *not* a wild pig. It is a hedgehog, small and prickly, and it rolls itself into a ball.'

'I guess, Arthur, he means a porcupine. Sounds to me like a porcupine.'

To me, and the rest of us, it all sounded the most good natured of madness as the talk flowed on the bell of closing time. And that was another thing which we had, and they apparently didn't!

CHAPTER TWELVE

HE LAST OVER

WHEN OUR NEIGHBOUR, Len, announced that he proposed to sell for five figures the modest residence for which he had paid a paltry hundred or two during the war years, a wave of anguish rolled over the Parish. Len, you see, was one of the most amenable of sinews which ever helped hold together a rural community. Len is bell-ringer, scrap dealer, cricketer, handyman, taxi driver, and, if sorely pressed, jobbing gardener. When in trouble – send for Len. That was the axiom by which the village had lived from the Rectory to the Manor. And now the unbelievable – Len was selling up.

'Len you can't – you're mad.'

'Mad, mate? What's mad about taking thirteen-five for a wormy old shack like mine? *They're* mad, not me. No, I been here long enough.'

'But, Len, where are you going to go?'

'Ah, now you're asking. Pal of mine's got a little workshop near Pilchester, empty flat over it – got a mind to go in with him. He says he could do with a hand. Rears chickens and turkeys, too.'

'But, Len – what about *us*?'

'Have to look after yourselves a bit more, won't you, mate?' said Len with a grin which practically linked together his batlike ears, adding, 'Oh, and by the way, didn't I hear you say that you were looking out for a hundred peg-tiles for that porch of yours, if ever you get around to having it built?'

'We-ell, yes, Len, I did happen to mention it, I think – not that I'm in any real hurry.'

'Well, you'd better make up your mind', said Len, 'because I know where they are, and if you don't have them, then I know somebody who will.'

The porch had been a dream for many a long year, but the peg-tiles were a fact. And the price for these ever decreasing rarities was laughably low. They arrived in a pick-up borrowed by Len from his brother-in-law. 'And if it's all the same to you', said Len, 'I'd rather have cash.'

Len would always 'rather have cash'. He carried it on his person, what's more, in mouth-watering rolls, holding it as a principle that a man was never to know when it might not come in handy. The quick deal was the best deal, he declared, and nothing talked louder than money. A market stallholder in Lincolnshire once off-loaded a stuffed owl upon Len. Len knew that the Vicar's lady collected owls and had been bewitched by them from girlhood. The transition was effected between Len and the Vicar in the churchyard one evening after bell-practice. 'Leonard Milliken, you are quite incorrigible', declared the Vicar, 'but I confess that the bird will make an acceptable addition to my wife's aviary. Two pounds, you say?'

'Thirty-five bob to you, Vicar'.

'No, Milliken, two pounds you said and two pounds you shall have. I am not one to rob a man of his proper profit. Oh, and since we are met, I wonder if you could give my motor mower a look over? The cutting edge would seem to have strayed a mite from the, er, straight and narrow, if you follow me. . .'

'I'll be round first thing in the morning, Vicar', said Len Milliken, adding the two crisp ones to the grimy wad in his pocket.

And now Len Milliken, dealer in free range eggs, hauler of motor cars out of flood-waters, tree planter, motor mechanic and house painter was to go. Some well-to-do young Londoner who played the piano and was Something-in-the-City would start souping up Len's place with patios, Italianate pergolas and bowed-out fenestration. Something very real was going to be missing from the community around the Parish Pump.

True it is that at the moment of writing 'Len's Place' is a battered island in the surrounding chaos of sand hills, brick piles, timber and cement mixers which proclaim the transformation of modest rural residence into a trendy little country seat. But Len, praise be, is still with us, installed now in the between-the-wars bungalow wherein his mother-in-law had had the tact to expire within a fortnight of contracts being exchanged. That ill wind (the lady was aged and ailing) blew much good to a rural community, and Len's new workshop of cedar wood out at the back is a pleasure to behold.

Life around the Parish Pump goes on.

So, too, does the summertime appearance of that evergreen subject of conversation and disputation, the *rara avis*. The unusual fowl of the air at the bottom of somebody's garden, or seen flying across the road at chest level.

'I saw the most *extraordinary* bird yesterday – perhaps *you* can tell me what it is. I know you're an expert on such things. . .'

As a matter of fact, this writer is not an ornithologist by calling, but only a country-loving scribe who is often tempted, when rare birds are reported, to resort to the blank and bleak dismissal of the whole futile maunderings of bird identification by saying tersely, 'It was a duck'.

But there has suddenly been an eruption around the rural district of wildly unidentifiable birds. '*Describe* it? Well, it was about the size of a thrush – maybe a little bigger. It had a black head and a long curved beak. Its breast was a sort of reddish colour, and when it flew off it had a fan-tail with yellow streaks and a white patch on its back. I've never seen anything quite like it. Now what would that be?'

'It didn't have a crest by any chance?'

'A crest? Well, sort of, I suppose. It might have had, but it flew off so quickly that I didn't have time . . . yet, wait a moment, come to think of it, it *did* have a crest, a little one – at least, my husband thought it did.'

'Sounds to me as though you might have had a hoopoe. And if it *was* a hoopoe, that *is* news.'

Hoopoe? Oh! No. Peewit for sure.

Always the mysteries of the rare bird reports remain unresolved. Birds that were 'a sort of greeny-brown with a pink patch on either cheek': birds 'about the size of a sparrow, marked like a swallow and with a long narrow tail': birds 'flying in spirals and whistling – no, definitely *not* a lark – who ever heard a lark whistle?'

The mind goes back to a bleak January day many years ago when a bird-minded – but far from bird-brained – lady telephoned from a nearby village seeking my 'expert confirmation' that a Siberian

Tit was wintering in her garden. It had been around for all of a fortnight. 'The whole village', she cried, 'is *throbbing* with excitement about this tit of mine.'

I was able to put her in touch with a true-blooded ornithologist who came, and saw, and declared that the lady was dead right. It *was* a Siberian Tit, though the village was too occupied otherwise to 'throb with excitement' when the presence of the visitor was recorded in an ornithological journal.

If there be a dramatic memory of Junetide to carry over into the sultry sun and thunder of dark-leaved July, let it be the last over of the Sunday cricket match on the sward of Parson's Green, a Chapel-minded community only persuaded within recent years to concede desecration of the Sabbath to the pressure of a squire-archical group. There is no pavilion between the great elm trees which line one side of the cricket ground – only *The Jolly Waggoners* public house which does duty as changing room. A trestle table outside serves for scorers beside the flimsy score board on a pole.

Stumps to be drawn at seven o'clock precisely, at *which* precise time the Baptist minister had given notice of his intention to hold an open-air service, complete with harmonium, right outside *The Jolly Waggoners.*

Five minutes to seven, last over to be bowled, last pair in, eighty six on the board, two runs for a home-side win, harmonium in position and the Baptist minister himself seen to be examining the score books with an interest not wholeheartedly spiritual. Two runs for a home win, eh? Our own Laurie Parkiss putting down two straight on a length up to the batman. A third wide of the leg stump, a windmilling hook and the ball beating wicket-keeper for one bye. One to win, three balls to come, and our Laurie pounding up to the wicket for the first of them. No strike. Scores level at eighty seven, and, yes, visible beads of perspiration on the brow of the Baptist minister. Fifth ball of the over, and the minister nodding towards the hands of Miss Pettigrew upraised above the keyboard of the harmonium. A bouncer, trapped high by wicket-keeper. One to come, and down it came, the Yorker which spreadeagled all three stumps behind the Parson's Green batsman. A tie!

Then everything that could dramatically happen happened on the instant. First stroke of seven from the distant church clock, first lowly notes from Miss Pettigrew's harmonium, and, as though this were not enough, over the green in line ahead came its rightful possessors, farmer Grimsby's half-dozen geese. This, too, was the fortuitous moment for three painted Gipsy caravans to process grotesquely picturesque, along the lane at the very far side of Parson's Green.

Geese, harmonium, church clock, a tied match. It was almost too much to coincide with the moment when *The Jolly Waggoners* ceased to be a pavilion and became a pub.

If ever a summer's day rang up the perfect curtain to the evening of its last act it was this one upon a foreign field just three miles from the Parish Pump.

CHAPTER THIRTEEN

THE UNOFFICIAL PARLIAMENT

THERE IS, I am glad to say, still one 'two up and two down' in the Parish which has not been acquired as a weekend retreat by a London business man, colour-washed, re-fenestrated, retiled, new-plumbed and fitted out with a car port or garage for the Jag. 'Meadowsweets' would most likely have been the name bestowed by such an owner upon Charley and Kate Cutler's place which, if it required identification at all, is now very properly known as 'Cutler's' as, I understand, it has been for all of a century. 'Cutler's up Gravel Lane' is the manner in which Charley and Kate's residence is described to any enquiring stranger, and heaven knows there are few enough of those to care about Charley and Kate.

'Cutler's' under its mossy thatch might have been painted by any skilful nineteenth century lady water colourist. Thatch, hollyhocks, sunflowers in season, cobbled pathway with, upon either side of it, the brilliant floral muddle of Kate Cutler's husbandry. Old-fashioned flowering things – sweet william, anemone, snapdragon, windflower, pansy, verbena, candytuft and marigold. Kate Cutler, watched by her two fat cats, seems simply to scratch around like an old hen in her pleasance for things to grow in proper season, seed themselves and reappear in an apparently weedless higgledy-piggledy. There is, of course, a honeysuckle covering half the cottage, and sweet geranium in every downstairs window – all two of them.

Behind 'Porson's' is Charley's immaculate kitchen garden, and at the end of that, under the summer froth of that exuberant climber styled 'Mile-a-Minute', is very properly an old-fashioned privy. The whole set-up, chicken run, rabbit hutches and all, belongs to another age.

Long ago, when I was very new beside the Parish Pump, Charley Cutler, then farm worker in his early forties, would 'give me', as they say, four hours weekly of his summer evenings to, as *he* would say, 'help ye out' in my garden. With vegetables he was a natural; for flowers he had no time.

'You don't want to go having all they', he would say, looking sourly at the waste space of my herbaceous plants. 'What you want 'stead of they's a good spread of spuds as ye can clamp up for the winter, spring greens where ye got them fancy daisies and that over agin that little old apple tree, and a proper old onion bed in the middle. Flowers is like chickens, more trouble'n they're worth.'

Charley never did see any sense to flowers, but granted that they were all right in their place, like Kate's, in any little bit of garden front of the place. But the back of any place was for the filling of the household's belly. Over my many years in the village I have done monthly battle with Charley Cutler whose own battle-cry against any 'foreigner' who employs him opens up always with the injunction: 'You don't want to go having. . .'

A long time ago when he was working spasmodically at eliminating my next door neighbour's border of hardy annuals when my neighbour was on holiday. Charley, peering over the boundary hedge, observed my wife and me preparing a wide trench lined with clinker to uphold the notion of a gravel path.

'What d'ye think you're a doing of?' suddenly demanded Charley.

'Oh – hullo, Charley. Well, since you ask, we're going to lay a gravel path all along this side of the vegetable garden against the hedge.'

'Gravel *parth*? You don't want to go having no gravel *parth* up agin that hedge. What *you* want's a nice bit o' grass.'

'No, I don't, Charley. I want a gravel path.'

'I'm telling ye – what you want there's a nice bit o' grass.'

'Charley, I do *not* want a nice bit of grass. I want a gravel path – what's more, I'm going to mix in sodium chlorate with the gravel when I lay it. So?'

'Sodium whatsit or not, what you'll git there come a year or two's a bit o' grass anyway, so you might just as well start it off now.'

There was a kind of lunatic logic in this, since time, combined with a measure of indolence, caused the gravel path – dampish and out of view from the house – to fall into some neglect. It was not pure grass, but a creeping carpet of moss, twitch and other intrusive herbage which conquered the gravel path. 'I told ye', said Charley, who had by then abandoned part-time gardening for ever, and was well content to stroll about the Parish casting an eye of silent destructive comment at other parishioners' visible husbandry.

Charley is now one of the ancient men who are alas – the dwindling hard core of the tap-room of *The Star and Wheelbarrow*. Ancient men full of the guile, bigotry and prejudice which are built in to the old-style countrymen. Charley and Nathan, Josh and Matthew, village grandads, three of them with an Old Testamental flavour in their names. Male rustics are no longer named after the Prophets, though we have to admit a thirty-five-year-old Daniel, otherwise known as Dan, who is a mineral water sales representative, as fizzing as his products. Dan will never become a tap-room ancient man in the traditional meaning of the phrase. Although domestically a villager, Dan is part of the rushing new world which the true ancient men view with increasing dis-ease. Dan, upon a Saturday evening, takes his missus into the Saloon bar and buys her schooners of sherry, while he downs large 'Bloody Mary's'! Dan drives a Company Cortina. Not one of the ancient men – saving Josh who still maintains a thirty-three-year-old Ford 8 – has ever driven a car in his life.

'Moty cars! Ye can't see *The Star* Sundays for moty-cars.'

Their tap-room, the unofficial parliament, the meeting house of the Elders is changing all about them. Permissive-looking 'girlie' calendars seem to leer improperly at the ancient men, wobbling their bosoms and bottoms at them from the walls. A 'one arm bandit' rattles its nervous musketry against their deliberations. At dinnertime unthinking strangers dropping out of their firms' cars for pints and sandwiches seat themselves upon the time-honoured thrones of the ancient men – Josh's place at the fireside end of the settle, Matthew's at the dartboard end, Nathan's Windsor chair by the fire itself, and the shallow seat in the bay window, Charley's by right of long usage.

Worst evil of all for these rude four fathers of the future is the piped pop which comes and goes about their hairy old ears. From Nathan anent this intrusive rumpus came the comment which shall go into the 'unforgettables file'.

'A party', quoth Nathan, 'carn't hear hisself think.'

To Josh and Matthew, Charley and Nathan the tap-room of *The Star and Wheelbarrow* may have changed for the worse, but to the summertime wanderers from overseas it proclaims itself, as always, the practical materialisation of a dream. The village pub! Exactly as they had been told that it would be. It is all true, down to the room-temperature beer, the box of dominoes, the cribbage board, the high settle, the ancient men themselves. It is cute: it is great: it is *wunderschoen*: it is *une ambience vraiment rustique et convenable*.

The middle-aged American couple who turned up one lunchtime in a chauffeur-driven hire car had spent, with the Vicar and the Parish Register, a profitable hour ancestor hunting in the church-yard. For there beneath a lichened headstone wearing skull, cross-bones and the winged head of an angel spirit arising there lay the body of Nicholas Fairfeather, 'Departed this Life ye 5th Day of October 1778'. This was cause for rejoicing in *The Star and Wheel-barrow*, man-sized Scotch whiskies to the memory of that moulder-ing ancestor. 'I guess', said the husband, 'this makes me a native. Hi, fellas', he addressed the small company assembled, 'meet Joe Fair-feather from the State of Illinois. My grandfather always said that my folks came from here, and darned if he's not proved right.'

None present defaulted in the toast to the family Fairfeather.

This year no Fête was held within the Parish, but Great Seething up the road had theirs, and, little though we care for the big-headed folk of Seething, we had to give them high marks for their Fête. We went. We always do, if only for the Flower Show, juicy and beguiling in the month of roses, steepling with giant delphini-ums and muzzy with the fragrance of sweet peas. First Prize, Second Prize, Third Prize, Highly Commended, the proud coloured labels bestowed by the strictly impartial judges during their two hour private deliberations between twelve noon and two of the clock. Home made scones, sausage rolls, Victoria sponges; jams, preserves, chutneys and home made wines. With the explosion of this domestic industry aided by astute advertising and do-it-your-self tipple-making kits, an entry this year of daunting proportions – red currant and rhubarb, potato and parsnip, golden mead, bright dandelion, cowslip, wheat and elderflower.

Yes, for all their faults and *folies de grandeur* Great Seething put on a rich, and even genial, summer occasion. And when in late afternoon we returned to the environs of our own Parish Pump we were in close peril of actually loving the blighters!

CHAPTER FOURTEEN

T HE TAVERN IS THE BETTER FOR THEM

THE VILLAGE STREET – no true street, but a wide country lane
sprinkled with cottages and small houses – lies along the furrow of
what we call 'The Brook', and between two low loins of mild hills.
The hills to the west only begin to rise about half a mile from the
valley floor: those to the east begin their upwards slope quite
abruptly, reaching their summit ridge in well under the half mile.

Beyond the ridge is a chalky tableland of a few square miles
which falls in its turn to a deeper valley beyond and the escarpment
of a higher, bolder hill-range. Our hills are the merest pimples in
stature, but they wear their own modest splendour. Our 'tableland'
is not true downland, being three parts given over to corn. But a
fourth part is so chalky as to be not worth the cultivating. This
gives the feeling of a small-scale Sussex Down. The grass is short and
wiry, the pimpernel, trefoil and toadflax bloom, close-hugging the
ground. It is a place where larks possess the sky and, together with
the lapwing, lay their eggs in the thickets of low grass. It is a
hunting ground for the kestrels whose families for over twenty
years have been born and nested in the tallest of the three Scots
pines which stand in odd isolation upon almost the highest point of
the ridge. Who planted these strangers there, and why? With the
words: 'Being glad of you, O pine-trees and the sky', Rupert Brooke
ended one of his earliest and most poignant of love poems. Saving
the fact that *his* pine trees were at Lulworth, these three of ours
could be the very trees that gladdened the poet's young heart. My
own heart always gladdens at the sight of these dark solitaries, bent
slightly from west to east by the prevailing winds, their feet among
the July scabious and the winking wings of chalk-blue butterflies,

the lark song over, and all about their strong ankles the wayward droning of fat and furry humble-bees.

Once upon a time not all that long ago a small, rather scraggy and untended few acres of woodland lay against the side of the hill overlooking the village. A few fine trees there were, but most of the couple of acres of the little wood was rotting elder and the like. There was a moat amidships surrounding a low hillock, and something had once stood upon that hillock. Moat, hillock and wood were bulldozed for corn years ago, but before this happened visiting achaeologists had deemed moat and hillock to have been the site of a Saxon Mot-and-Bailey.

Now I remember the little wood for other aspects – for the wind-flowers and the bluebells of early summer and springtime, the cowslips about its margins, the rabbit warren on its southern rim, sun-facing and lively of a summer's evening with bobbing white tails and flurries of brown fur. Once the rough little wood was a natural meeting place for the lads and the lasses of the community around the Parish Pump.

It was in fact the 'Milk Wood' of the village, and most villages surely have one such! Thither went the 'Polly Garters' of the Parish either with, or to meet, their swains. 'When', as Dylan Thomas did indeed say, 'I was young and eager . . .' my respectable married eye dwelled from a distance upon the comely curves of one of those 'Polly Garters', and, being male and human, I had discreet envy for the Bens, and the Bobs, and the Teds who vied for the favours of Maureen Strang. For that was the name of the wayward little beauty. Maureen Strang. Ah, me! she was quite a girl, was Maureen. All of thirty years ago.

A few Saturday evenings back and I was seated in the evening summer sunshine upon one of the two benches outside *The Star and Wheelbarrow*. Beside me, pint in hand, was one of the very ancient men of the Parish. We sat and we watched the world going by, the visitors, the natives, the old, the 'any-ages', the young. The new style lads and lasses of the village in their figure-hugging jeans, their mutual plumages of hair. Where, the ancient man and I, 'standing on the corner', as the song said, 'watching all the girls go by.'

'Can't rightly tell which is which these days', said my aged companion. 'Not like they was in my young days. Always tell the difference, you could in them days.'

'I'm not your generation, Tom', said I, 'but you could tell the difference in *my* days, too. Remember Maureen Strang? She was a lass and a half around these parts.'

'Maureen?' quoth he, 'Her name weren't Maureen. It was Sarah, and *she* was a lass all right, you're right.'

'Tom, it was *not* Sarah – it was *Maureen* who was the one who led the boys on. Not that she ever led me on, though I wouldn't have minded, mind you! Oh, yes, I could have gone for Maureen, Tom. Remember the old wood?'

'*Course* I remembers the old wood. Great place for courting, the old wood. And Sarah – many's the time. . .' His voice dwindled away.

'Tom – haven't you got things a bit wrong? *Maureen* Strang . . .'

On the instant his old eyes filled with rheumy merriment, and the laughter came rumbling up from his belly.

'It's *you* what's got things a bit wrong, boy. Maureen, come to think of it, was Sarah's *daughter*. It was Sarah as I was a-thinking of. *Sarah* Strang. Oh! she was the one all right, was Sarah. . .'

The half-generation gap was clear as the dawn. I went in to *The Star* and replenished the pints. Well, well – Sarah and Maureen Strang – quite a couple of girls, the pair of them! Like mother, like daughter!

'They thinks these days', went on old Tom, hot on his subject, 'as they's the only ones what ever thought of malarkying about. They thinks as we was just a lot of goody-goodies in knickerbockers and pinafores when we was their age. All Boys' Brigade and Sewing Bees. But t'weren't like that, I can tell ye. Whoi, of a summertime there was a 'alf-dozen of us used to go a-bathing up Bramley Lake. Ever been up there? Tucked away it is, back of a coppice back of Bramley. We didn't trouble about no bathing costumes and that, and I tell ye as Sarah Strang was the first as got her pinafore off, and all the rest of it besoides. . . Oh, them was the days. . .'

Sarah Strang, come to think of it, was a frowsty bundle of middle-aged jellybag when first I came to the village and had eyes only for buxom Maureen. She, too, I dared say, went swimming with the lads up Bramley Lake and wasn't slow to be rid of her cotton frock.

Plus ça change, plus c'est la même chose!

Now in and around *The Star and Wheelbarrow*, and especially about Saturday dinnertimes, the youth of the village is very much in evidence, patched jeans, bushshirts and all. 'Just a lot of long-haired layabouts, those young men', snorted a certain spinster of this Parish recently, 'and as for some of the girls, they seem to have no sense of shame. Take that little minx, Sandra Bilton. Why, she doesn't even wear a *brassière*.'

No, she doesn't, and young Peter Sanders with his beard, shoulder-long hair, tattooed arms, bared chest, and figure-hugging gear doesn't leave much to the imagination. But up with such remarks as those of that spinster of the Parish I will not put. Peter and Sandra, Linda and Joe, Laurie Spratt, Stan Porson, Robbie Grigg, Myrtle and Miriam and the Clegg sisters, are a great bunch of kids. I love their laughter of a Saturday morning, the lads with their lights and bitters, the girls with their Rum-and-Cokes, gin-and-bitter-lemons and lager-and-limes. Maureen and her mum, Sarah, would never have dared lighten the doors of the old *Star*. Linda and Sandra and Myrtle and Miriam *do*. And the tavern is the better for them, save sometimes when they turn up their ten pennorths of juke-box a bit loud. Peter Sanders, the brawny bare-chested cowman up at The Manor, is generally the first to say 'Bit on the loud side for you, mate? Sorry. I'll turn it down.' They work hard, they play hard, they laugh loud, these 'long-haired layabouts', and I have all the time in the world for them.

Their idiom may differ markedly from that of more senior citizens of the Parish, but what of it? It doesn't make it any the nastier. In many ways it is more concise and explicit.

'You hot-rodding Sunday, Peter?'

'Can't make it, mate. Me "Rod's" blown a gasket. Sandra and me's taking a quiet road-ride over to Bilberry to see her mum.'

Get it? Message loud and clear.

There is, alas, no old 'Milk Wood' any more up to which Sandra and Pete might have taken their summer evening way, past the rabbit warren and in among the wood sorrel by the moat where the moorhens and the dabchicks once cruised with their young families. They would, I fancy, be unlikely too to press on further over the lip of the hill, across the tableland where the larks hang high, and foot it past the lone pines to the tiny coppice of wych-elm, young beech and sycamore which lies beyond.

'Bit of a drag footing it all that way, Sandy.'

Yes, quite. None the less, surely worth the footing. If only to smell the wind on the heath, and listen to the yell of the yaffle as, like a green and scarlet undulating rocket, he flies from the coppice to a perch upon a solitary pine.

'Yes, Pete. Let's get the old banger out and go over to Mum's for tea.'

Great kids, all the same.

CHAPTER FIFTEEN

*L*OVE THY NEIGHBOUR

IT MUST BE true of all villages that nothing excites more than new neighbours – unless it be some spectacular misdemeanour among old ones. 'Miss Enderby – Miss *Enderby!* But I simply can't *believe* it. She's such a quiet, mousy little thing. No, no, it can't be true.'

But we devoutly hope that it is!

We fancy that we know all the essentials of old neighbours, but new ones are charged with mysterious potential – like Jake, the genial, unquiet American who came some years back with his wife and young family to live for two years among us, and left behind him an affection which still lives in an afterglow of his warm humanity about the long thatched cottage called 'Starlings'.

But more of Jake by and by. It is the newly arrived residents in 'Starlings' which intrigue and perplex us – the Wholeheartedlys with their mariegold-finish Toyota car, their bull mastiff called 'Gunner' and the contrived patina with which they have overlaid the social image of their partnership. This is the couple which perplexes and intrigues. Are they a true bill of cordial concord, or a pair of outrageous *flâneurs* to be trusted no further than the camellia which was the first thing that Emerald Wholeheartedly planted by the front door of 'Starlings' in early November, swearing that it would be a mass of creamy bloom by mid-summer?

From time to time when they were negotiating for the purchase of 'Starlings' and bringing round surveyors and architects to talk about it, the Wholeheartedlys popped into *The Star and Wheelbarrow* for lunchtime bread and cheese and beer. We eyed them warily, Jocelyn Wholeheartedly, forty-fiveish, well cut sky-blue

74

pants, linen shirt and wolfish grey hair. Mrs W., with an 'interesting' face, not unlike that of a woolly monkey, blue jeans, polo neck jersey and twitchy, nervous hands. Early forties. What the French call a '*jolie-laide*'. Their movements were mondaine and sophisticated, and they wore freshly disarming smiles.

There was no question of the Wholeheartedlys not speaking unless spoken to. 'I think I'd better warn you', said Jocelyn W., addressing a couple of us old inhabitants who chanced to be present, 'that we're the new boy and girl who've bought "Starlings" up the road. I hope you'll find us not too dreadful to put up with – or should I say "up with whom to put"?'

This was a far from diffident first approach, and it became even farther when he continued, 'The name's Wholeheartedly, I'm afraid, but we just can't help that. This is my wife, Emerald, and I'm Jocelyn, and I can't help that either. I think it's difficult to believe in a couple called Emerald and Jocelyn, but there it is – our friends call us the "Wholesomes". I'm the "some" part. And I promise you that I'm not trying to be funny when I say that I do actually come from Somerset, you know. I can't help that, either – can I, darling?'

'There are lots of things you can't help, you poor pet', said 'Whole'.

'Be that as it may, but, anyway, for better or worse, here we are – scared stiff of everybody, of course, but we'll do our best to be good neighbours.'

That, in the manner which made us wince slightly, was curtain-up in the drama of the newcomers which still goes on. Were they – are they – a pair of name-dropping line shooters, a couple of culture snobs with all their talk of 'Willie' Walton, Alec Douglas-Home, 'Laurie' Durrell and his crazy brother, 'Frankie' Bacon and the jet set on Sardinia?

'Some' asked about the shooting, saying that he wished to do honour to his Purdey gun, while 'Whole' was anxious to carry on with her flower-arranging studies and admitted to 'dabbling in oils' in a small way. They had a son whom they called 'our poor, hopeless Nicholas', and 'Some', speaking of the bull mastiff 'Gunner', described him as 'Toad-Dog' and spoke gaily and convincingly of the breeder from whom they had bought him in Northamptonshire.

But all this was – and still is – proclaimed with decent discretion,

75

and we cannot but like the Wholeheartedlys. A little bit of quiet needling has shown beyond doubt that they truly *do* know the Douglas-Home country, down to the whiskered landlord of a mutually known pub. Sir William Walton's home on Ischia was spot on–I've been there; and 'Whole's' dabbling in oils is far more than a joke. What's more, I've *seen* the Purdey gun, been gently nipped by 'Gunner' and listened to 'Some's' railway recordings on his Hi-Fi Stereo.

The fellow is something in the field of Industrial Public Relations, and when he says that he's had to go to Thurso for a few days we have no reason to doubt him. Though sometimes, in grimy denims and a turtle-neck sweater, he's around the Parish Pump for days and has even been accepted in the hierarchical tap-room of '*The Star and Wheelbarrow*'.

They still remain, in their unruffled bonhomie and united front, something of a mystery. Almost too good to be true. But after nearly six months we have come to believe that they are. They are 'cards', they are '*numeros*', and, let us parochially face it – definite assets.

'Starlings', over the years, has had some rum customers within its timbered walls. The stout Scottish lady doctor and her highly strung friend, Miss Grisby; the self-consciously 'truly rural' family the Strongbows, defiantly churning their own butter, baking their own bread, growing their own tobacco and getting clearly sozzled on their home made rhubarb and elderflower wines. The year-long 'furnished let' stay of the bearded architect, Amos Grimbleton, with his overt penchant for Peggy the post girl. All but Peggy-the-Post were pleased to see the back of Amos, and the smell of his herbal tobacco in the pub.

But of all the incumbents of 'Starlings', a breath of uninhibited reality after the musty old poseur Amos, the richest was Jake from the State of Michigan. Jake – christened Jaques – had a plump little wife, Bettina, and two sublime little girls, one fat as butter, the other wan, slender and beautiful in the mould of Alice in Wonderland. And to these two little American girls the lanes, the coppices, the meadows and the brook around our Parish Pump became, indeed, a wonderland which they have never forgotten.

The family were fine, and Jake was the finest. He had been invalided out of the American Navy with a head wound and a pension. 'I caught my war wound playing soft ball', explained Jake.

Straight from the U.S.Navy he went to University, studying History, Philosophy and the Celtic peoples. He married. He got himself a Fulbright grant for two years post graduate study at our nearby senior University. And, lock stock and barrel, he moved Bettina and the kids into that seventeenth century cottage, 'Starlings' in the unknown ambience of a truly English village.

Jake was tall, lean, rangy as a hairpin. He shambled a bit. When he first shambled into '*The Star and Wheelbarrow*' to meet that deadly hush which always falls upon village tap-rooms when a stranger enters he said: 'Hi! Jeez, it's true, it's *true*, just like they told me it was – a village pub. My name's Jake Delaroy, and I just moved in to "Starlings" up the road. Will somebody tell me what's the best beer to drink around here?'

We told him. 'The bitter', we said.

'You'll have to forgive my ignorance, fellers', said Jake, 'I'm really raw around these parts, but I'm ready to learn and I want to learn.'

And he learnt! With civilised charm and humility, Jake quietly integrated himself into the great unknown of the English country-side. He bought an old 'Banger' and drove daily to his studies. He asked endless, searching questions about everything. It was April when he shambled on to the cricket meadow to watch evening net practice.

He gazed for some time in a kind of stunned silence. And then he said: 'I don't get it – I just don't get it. Does the pitcher always just *bounce* the ball to the batter?'

'Always – that's the point, Jake.'

'Then he's not pitching?'

'No – he's bowling.'

'Just let me get in there with a bat', said Jake, 'and I'll tag the ball out of the lot.'

We let him take strike. We let loose upon his rangy innocence our leg-spinner, Gerry Meadows. Jake struck. His stumps were hit four balls out of seven. He contacted once. 'Jeez', he said, 'I get it – that ball doesn't bounce the way it should. . .'

In a month Jake was turning out for the village. 'It's the game', he said, 'It's *the* game. Why, baseball, softball's kids' stuff to this.'

He was a hopeless batsman. In the field he was a greyhound. He threw into the wicket as a pitcher born. He revelled in it all, and we revelled in him.

77

Impossible in these so few lines to evoke the charm, the warmth and the wisdom of Jake Delaroy, our unquiet American. It was probably because he loved us and our, to him, crazy slow way of life, that we loved him. It is good to be loved.

On hot summer evenings he would often poke his head round the corner of the cottage and say, 'Hi, there – I've just fixed some juleps – come and help us drink them under the old apple tree, huh?'

What evenings they were with the juleps under the old apple tree at 'Starlings'. Jake and Bettina. 'I guess, Betsy', he said one evening, 'I guess you and me's going to stop right here for the rest of our lives. Hell! I'm practically Limey right now.'

Of course, in time they went. But still something more than the ghost of them clings around 'Starlings' and the Parish Pump.

CHAPTER SIXTEEN

HARVEST DAYS

I SHALL NEVER forget the spectacle of my son bursting into the kitchen on that burnished August late afternoon of many years gone. He was ten years of age, and he wore shorts, a singlet and a pair of gym shoes. Arms and legs were burned to the colour of a nectarine, covered with scratches from encounters with hedgerows and harvest. His pale, upstanding hair was full of the dust and débris of the harvest field, and he radiated the sunshot excitement of the afternoon. He carried a stub of blackthorn in one hand, and from the other, upheld in all the triumph which lies in the heart of the hunter, there dangled the furry small carcase of a stoat. Sad stoat.

'I – I saw him, and, and – I chased him – and I got him', cried my son.

'Poor old stoat', I said. 'What are you going to do with him, now that you've killed him?'

'*Do* with him? I'm – I'm going to have him skinned, and, and, he'll make a super fur for mummy.'

Ten days later sad stoat, stinking and humming with blowflies, was hooked from its nail at the back of the garden shed, and deftly interred behind the compost heap.

The image of that faraway August day of harvest remains forever in my mind – in the mind, too, of the son now with a son of his own. *He* has never forgotten the sun-bitten day of the stoat, the day when reaper and binder had gone out upon the forty-acre field on the hillside. Before then men with scythes had swathed down the headlands of the field and hand-tied the sheaves already standing upon them.

79

Early in the morning of that golden day, its hedgesides braided with bird's-eye, pimpernel, toadflax and campion, reaper and binder set forth, tractor-hauled after years of horses, binder sails seeming to reap the very blue of the sky, while the cutting blade rasped down the standing corn. Coarse twined, the sheaves were cast upon the stubble, and men following the binder upended sheaves into stooks to ripen in the sun and cast down, in absolute beauty, their long shadows in early evening for the September days to come.

Late, late in the afternoon reaper and binder had closed in upon the centre of the field, the last square of standing corn. Now the dramatic tragedy, the inevitable closing ceremony, never now seen as combine harvesters, like painted dinosaurs, chumble up and down the harvest fields. Mind you, I'm not sure about this. Perhaps, in its own way, that final tragedy still does take place – the last rush for shelter of the last wild things confined in the standing corn. But I doubt whether there are that many wild things left to rush, or anyone interested enough to pursue them.

But back to the day of the stoat. In that last square of upright wheat were potential dinners – fat rabbits, hares and leverets, maybe a game-bird, though neither Matthew nor Charley with their four-tens would dare take a public pot at partridge or pheasant late in August. Apart from the two guns waiting by the coppice for the dinners to run over the stubble straight towards them, there were the farm workers with thick cudgels, and a cluster of excited kids bidden to keep well clear of the coppice. And among them, ten years of sheer boy, my son with his blackthorn stub.

Smaller and smaller the dwindling sanctuary, until at last – out, hither and thither, the poor, panicked wildlings rushed, quite a dozen rabbits, a hare, three leverets, the ginger pencil of a weasel, a grass snake and, of course, the stoat! A 'paff' and a 'paff', a concerted shouting, a whacking, a running, a thumping, and it was all over – total bag two shot rabbits, four clobbered rabbits, and a grass snake mercilessly pulped for no reason other than that it was a snake. And the stoat. Hare and leverets clear away.

It's not difficult to maunder nostalgically about old-time harvest days around the Parish Pump. They *were* more parochially personal, more dramatic, more picturesque – and less efficient – than the mechanised matter-of-factness of today. Other-day harvests chattered lightly about the landscape. Today's go over it, thumping and thundering as the instant golden grain pours from the back of the combine. A quarter of a century gone, and the stooks stood at leisure in the ripening sun, until pitch-forked, sheaf by sheaf, into trailer or wain. The last load home came to the stacks with song, and sprays of oak leaves – 'Oakey' – crowned it. At leisure, too, and in their own good time, the hired threshing tackles came to the farmyards, to fill them with the lazy and falling hum as the sheaves, in irregular batches, floated to the threshing drum upon the elevator. The dust and the chaff flew all about, and the oily, smoky steam engines, flywheels spinning, drove the threshing tackle with great leather belts.

Within not many miles radius there were several entrepreneurs with tackle and steam traction for hire, complete with the sleeping vans for attendant crews. The engines and tackle steamed many miles from farm to farm and, in the Dormy vans, the crews slept on the job.

I am pretty certain that the steam traction which came annually to the stackyard just back of the Parish Pump upon its triangle of green was by Fowler of Leeds.

In the second half of the nineteenth century the coal fired, deep-chested agricultural monsters by Fowler of Leeds began to revolutionise agricultural methods. Fowlers rolled roads, drove threshing tackle and, in majestic pairs, ploughed fields. Many wore muscular names in brass letters upon their boilers – Victory, Samson, Goliath, Hercules, Fury.

During this very midsummer four twenty-ton Fowlers arrived upon a fifty-acre field which had been shorn of its mixed fruits of rye grass, clover and lucerne. These four Behemoths were engaged in a whole weekend's demonstration of steam ploughing and cultivating, fifteen pence to watch it, hot dogs, fish and chips and soft drinks available. Many from the village drove just over the chalk ridge to behold the spectacle, and an impressive fifteen penn'orth it was.

'Victory' at work made diesel traction look like a Triang toy. 'Victory' weighed twenty tons and, on a hard day's work, would burn a ton of coal and swallow a thousand gallons of water. Likewise her distant team-mate at the far headland of the field. Beneath each belly of 'Victory' and her mate a colossal steel drum of wire cable. Between the pair of them a double-sided six-furrow plough weighing three tons, shares pointing fore and aft – one set ploughing a foot deep as hauled by 'Victory', the other clear of the stubble but ready to be lowered when it was the turn of 'Victory's' mate to haul the plough back. Both engines chuntering a new six furrow's width for the return trip, squealing to each other the code whistles for 'all set'.

'Victory' was jet black, her tall chimney collared with bright brass. Her deep-ribbed iron driving wheels were nearly seven feet in diameter. Her fly-wheel spun at two hundred revolutions a minute, so fast as to appear stationary. Her double-expansion cylinders poured power into the sleek and oily pistons. Her engineer, dark with coal dust, his boiler-suit shining with oil and an oily cap upon his head, was quite a young fellow. He grinned, laughed and sang as he slammed through his charge's colossal gears, and pulled the cord which sent 'Victory' screaming across that sun-smitten, smoke-smelling, oil-scented hillside.

'Ah, but she's a lady – a real lady', observed one elderly clergyman to another.

'Fowler could breed them', replied the other.

What was it, I wondered, as I saw the admiring eye of yet another dog-collared attendant upon one of the other great steamers, which draws the clergy so compulsively to old traction, old cars, old paddle-steamers, old trains? Almost any Branch Line Preservation Society, I'm sure, will feature a parson on its committee. When the Flying Scotsman made her nonstop London to Edinburgh run, there were parsons in every coach.

Perhaps it is simply that, like so many of us, they revere the romance of steam power. Only, being in uniform, they are the more noticeable.

Like ageing prima donnas the great engines sang their arias to a pop-eyed audience. There were film cameras, ordinary cameras, young men watching the 'modding' of the needles on their tape recorders. And, scattered here and there about the crowds, ancient men of steam (retired). There was a party of four of these old timers sinking pints in *The John Barleycorn* back in the local village. They recalled great feats of other days. 'We started up five o'clock in the morning', said one, 'and by seven we'd finished up eighty acres, cultivating. 'Course, we wuked them days, twelve hours and more was nothing.'

'They don't know what wuk is these days', said another.

'It'd do some of these young tractor fellers good to keep a six-furrow steady atween a pair of "sheens". Ploughing! They gits down six or seven inches and they calls it ploughing. We used to get down a foot or more.'

That was one summer's highlight to be remembered among a fair galaxy around the Parish Pump. Frank Saunders flashing 132 not out in the first of the two Great Seething 'Derby' matches, and the fact that we won both. The Horticultural Society's Annual Fruit, Flower and Vegetable Show, with the so-called 'impartiality' of the judges a mockery when it came to Farmer Hickory's wife, Hetty, sweeping the floral board again. Who didn't know that Jack Juxon, Judge from Lower Muttering, was Hetty's brother, and Peter Sandon of Berry Green her brother-in-law! The Fête, we all agreed, had got itself into a groove, no originality, the same old goldfish goggling in their jam jars, the eternal bowling for the eternal pig, bottle stall, darts for the cockerel, buried treasure, hoop-la – the recipe as before.

Next year we *must* inject some ginger into that Fête of ours. But I doubt if we will.

Now once again September comes – spider-spin, dahlias, opening daisies of Michaelmas; manna of meadow mushrooms, fat marrows, swallows like music written upon the wires; and harvest chumbling trailed home without a single oak leaf upon the final load. Soon the wheat straw will rib the stubble with lines of flickering flame, and much life will be extinguished.

The mind returns to the day of the stoat, to the plumes of smoke from 'Victory' upon her sunny hillside of high summer. An unhealthy nostalgia for the flavour of things past? Unhealthy? Why? As well call unhealthy the memory of Wally Hammond punching them through the covers and saying, 'By heaven! there was a mighty batsman for you.'

Just as we may toast the memory of Walter Hammond, Headley Verity and John Berry Hobbs, so too may we raise a glass to 'Victory' by John Fowler of Leeds.

CHAPTER SEVENTEEN

Sam Whortle A-Bowling

IT IS PLEASANT of a September's Sunday afternoon to take position near the pavilion upon the cricket meadow close to the two benches on which the ancient men of the Parish perch for pronouncement. The season draws towards its close. Shadows of flannelled fools grow longer after teatime, and the swallows are gathering on the wires. Some of them on blue-bladed wings skim low over the field of play if the air is humid and the evening hatch of flies be thick at ground level.

Village cricket! It has all been said before, but let it be said again that there is a lambent melancholy which attends these last matches of the summertime. Already the footballers are getting fidgetty, but not the ancient men at perch as close of play draws near to coincide with the single church bell calling the faithful to Evensong.

The chief concern of the ancient men is to denigrate the puny midgets of the modern game and to exalt the Goliaths of other days.

'If they calls that faarst', says Nathan to Arch, 'whoi, they never seen Sam Whortle a-bowling, that's whoi. Sam Whortle was faarst, real faarst. Oi moind the toime when Sam Whortle broke the middle stump of one of they Spindleberry fellows like as if it had been a matchstick. Broke it clean in 'alf, Sam Whortle did.'

'Aaar', replies Arch, ''e really were faarst, were Sam Whortle, not loike what they calls faarst these days. 'E could've played for the County if he'd 'ad a moind to, could Sam. Faarst as Kortright, oi reckon.'

The imagination is stirred at this evocation of the mighty Sam Whortle, six foot three of him, thundering down the hill, eyes blazing with hatred for the trembling batsman at the receiving end of that whistling leather cannon-ball. But was it just possible that that shattered middle stump was a rotten yellow bone of a thing which had been standing for a full quarter of a century of summers up there on the cricket meadow? Was Sam really all *that* fast?

Now Nathan and Arch are at it again, this time on the subject of today's so-called batsmen – 'Scratchin' and pokin' about loike as if they was afraid o' their own shadders. Whoi, ye never see one of these fellers really clout the ball like what Aaron Higgs used to do. 'E really hit the ball, did Aaron.'

'Aaar, 'e were a proper little old clouter, were Aaron. Many a toime as I seen him hit one roight over that little old oak tree, crorst o' the road and twenty yards into Fifteen Acre Medder. Ye don't get that sort o' thing happening these days.'

'Ben Grunter, 'e were another loike what ye don't get today. Remember the toime Ben carted one clean through the winder o' "Woodside Cottage" what used to stand where the Council Houses stands now? But moind you, Ben weren't quoite in the class o' Aaron. Look at that feller out there now – seems as he thinks more to 'is fancy cap as 'e thinks to the cricket. Allus tweakin' at it. . .'

The ancient men are unimpressed by the fact that the cricket meadow of today is tailored and trim as a bowling green, that the well-prepared properly marled wicket plays true as many a County ground and that it is not uncommon for four hundred or so runs to be scored in an afternoon. And they have no respect for spotless flannels and 'fancy caps', even though these last may occasionally denote membership of clubs as distinguished as The Free Foresters or The Butterflies.

A mere twenty five years or so back, and we played with an outfield uncut, cattle running free and a Sunday morning labour force hard in the wake of the cattle with barrows, shovels and spades. What, then, were things like when Sam Whortle cannon-balled them down the wicket in the early twenties, and Aaron and Ben clouted them over oak and ash and cottage rooftop?

And what, to get to the truth of things, were Sam, Aaron and Ben really like – as cricketers?

That Score Book for the year 1921 took quite a lot of finding on the part of the Club Secretary, but find it he did for me. I was not acting in any unscrupulous manner in proclaiming my natural interest in the Club's past and had no intention of ever revealing to the ancient men what I found therein! Let, in fact, sleeping Sams, Bens and Aarons lie.

In 1921, it appeared, the great Sam Whortle bowled in eleven matches for a total of 112 overs. He was no-balled nine times, delivered six wides and dismissed twenty nine batsmen at an average of eighteen runs per victim. With the score for a whole innings rarely reaching more than seventy runs, Sam would seem quite right in not seeking that County Trial 'if he'd had a mind to'.

And how about that thick-thewed rural Jessop, Aaron Higgs? Twelve times did Aaron turn out for the village in 1921. Thrice he failed to score, but his highest score of twenty three upon August Bank Holiday did, indeed, include three sixes – his only sixes of the season. On four occasions he contrived to hit or tread upon his own wicket. The mighty Aaron's average was just a shade over six.

Yet the mind's vision of these giants, clouting and cannon-balling among the buttercups, cowpats and daisies remains warm and loving, and who but an incorrigible and heartless cad could produce the chilling evidence of that Score Book before the misty eyes of Nathan and Arch upon their bench? No, no – let Aaron, Sam and Ben rest for ever in glory.

'Thanks for the loan, Mr Secretary – most interesting.'

The church bell tolls towards the start of prayer and close of play, and that popinjay in the fancy cap has had the effrontery to carry his bat for sixty three runs. *The Star and Wheelbarrow* opens its evening doors, and still there are holidaymaking strangers pulling up for pints and seeking directions from the parishioners as to how best to proceed from here to there.

'Er – I wonder – could you tell me the best way to get to Ravening?'

If there's anything truly liable to arouse good-natured dissension in Saloon Bar or Tap-room of *The Star*, then it's the 'best way to get' business.

'Ravening, sir? Dead easy. Your's the Volvo Estate out there? Right, carry straight on the way you're facing, *through* the village, take the right fork after a big Dutch barn you'll see on the left – then straight as you can go, ignoring a couple of left turn-offs, for Pipley. Next *right*'ll take you to the Mutterings, and Ravening's some five miles west out of Lower Muttering – you'll see it marked...'

The strangers begin to mutter – 'right fork – two left turns *not* for turning – then the, what did you say. . .?'

'Right for the Mutterings, then steady as you go. . .'

The strangers at the bar are trapped between Joe who has issued these directions and Pete who shouts across them at Joe: 'What you want to send them all round by the Mutterings for, mate? You're mad. Best way to Ravening's straight through Steepleborough – what you want to send them all round the houses for? Now look, sir, don't you take any notice of what Joe here's said – if you'll take my advice you'll go left at the end of the village for Steepleborough.'

'That's all of three miles longer'. barks Joe.

'It's all of three miles prettier', says Pete. 'The Mutterings is dumps, and well you know it. The Steepleborough way takes them through Potter's End, and I reckon there's no prettier village in the County'n Potter's End. . .'

The eyes of the travellers glaze over as they look from Joe to Pete, from Pete to map and back again to Joe. They'll be lucky if they don't get our landlord, leaning quietly and confidentially across the bar and saying: 'If you'll excuse me, sir – and I go over to Ravening twice every week of my life – *I'd* say by far your best way, *and* the prettiest, is by way of Chevening. It means doubling back for about a mile the way you've come and going right for Chough-Chevening-Ravening – it's the back doubles, but well worth it. . .'

'Er – thanks – thanks very much, all of you – er – goodnight.'

And into a wilderness of their own devising drive the visitors, wishing to heaven that they'd kept their mouths shut. The discussion of ways and means they have left behind them will reach far into the night, gathering depth and dimension as it goes!

Meantime as dusk turns to the darkness of a September night about the Parish Pump it is pretty certain that, for the travellers, all charms of Chevenings, Mutterings, Choughs, Potter's End or what have you will be visible by headlights only!

CHAPTER EIGHTEEN

LIFE'S ONE LONG HOLIDAY

'COURSE, YOUR LIFE'S just one long holiday', proclaim certain grand old men of the soil who dwell within a few bucket-lengths of the long dry Parish Pump. Some trendy younger ones with bushy whiskers and Company cars are prone to cast at me similar jibes, poor home-based scribbler that I be, seen frequently out of 'working hours', lowering a pint in *The Star and Wheelbarrow*. Sometimes I depart from the village for a day or two on journalistic, and other, assignments which take me to exciting venues such as Scunthorpe, South Wales or, should I strike lucky, maybe the Scottish Borders or the silvery watersides of the River Wye.

'Off on your holidays again, I see', jeer the ancient men, who do not behold the brain-bashing within a head beaten into the awful discipline of a typewriter in a small back room. 'Wuk' not to be seen to be done is not 'wuk' at all, so, naturally, my life is one long holiday.

'See you're doing a mite of wuk for a change' observed one loamy old joker, chancing to pass me by as I was bedding out some stringy-looking asters in the front of the cottage.

Why try to point out that this back-breaking exercise is a bizarre kind of relief from what goes on indoors? 'That's right, Nathan', I replied, 'doing a little work, as you rightly observe.'

'I see you got suckers on all them roses o' yourn' ', came the parting shot as my derisive neighbour passed upon his way.

Now that it is September again, with the last trailer loads of tawny grain jolting along the lanes, the swifts long departed from the skies and swallow families chittering on the wires, the whole community seems to have been, is just gone, or is about to depart on holidays of a rangy flamboyance oddly at odds with other-day vacational exercises among dwellers about the Parish Pump.

True enough, Nathan has been traditionally to Clacton-on-Sea with the Over-Sixties in August, and the old Applejohns have been to share a chalet for a week with their son, daughter-in-law and grandchildren at Weston-super-Mare. And the Larks of the Post Office have been on a four-day coach trip to Wales. For a few traditional die-hards 'The Lights' at Blackpool or Southend remain as a last titbit before Christmas.

But the holiday exploits of such are very small potatoes compared with sun-smitten travelling of others at the end of a summer which started with 'Where you going for your holidays this year?', middled with 'had your holidays yet?', and has culminated with explosive and exuberant blow by blow accounts of thunderstorms on the Costa Brava, mosquitoes about the Costa del Sol and – 'it made my holiday' – the pinching of Lucy Fetlock's opulent bottom by the leader of an oompah band in Linz.

'Oh, but our coach driver was a scream – a positive scream – had us all in fits when we went to this lake place in Unterhausen, and there was this troupe of dancers, see, and Laurie – he was the driver – went up to one of the girls – mind you he'd had a few – and started to join in, see – it was a high-kicking sort of a dance, see, and she just did a double-quick turn, and fetched him one on the behind – *katchow*, just like that! Laugh, I thought we'd all have died. . .'

It's a wonder, indeed, that many of them didn't die when we hear blood-chilling reports of coaches missing precipices by inches in Norway, cable cars getting stuck halfway up the Drachenfels on the Rhine, and of Pete Harker's narrow escape from being clobbered in a Bierkeller rumpus in Munich. At this very moment of writing odd-jobbing builder Joe Cringle and his quiet little country mouse of a missus are on the eve of departing upon a whistle stop tour of 'Seven Romantic European Capitals in Ten Days'. We wish them the best of Parish luck, wondering how their digestions will deal with Rijstaffel in Amsterdam followed by sauerkraut and Bangers-of-the-Fatherland in Cologne.

Of course, as is only to be expected, the City folk who have made of the village a dormitory, have been escaping all this sort of thing in Sardinia, Crete and Corfu. But whatever the social level of the holidaymakers, the air about the Parish Pump has been throbbing, summerlong, with tales of the floating pound being torpedoed by the drachma and the Ibizan hotel which, far from floating, had not even been built!

In many ways I feel that the play-it-safe stay-at-homes have come off best, very especially old Amos Pilling, a daily scrutineer of the *Sporting Life* in the *Star and Wheelbarrow* tap-room, a dedicated follower of form and a great unimpressionable when horses, footballers and batsmen of today seem in any way to excel over those of yesterday.

Amos is a bachelor and a jobbing gardener, given to a daily investment of not more that 20p should anyone be 'getting through', to a bookmaker before the first race. A citizen of thrift and caution, a believer of cash in the pocket rather than pieces of paper in post offices or banks.

Here, then, was this pleasant summer's lunchtime in the taproom of *The Star and Wheelbarrow*, present being Amos and a fistful of other senior citizens together with two very junior ones – a pair of teenage maidens holidaymaking with their grandparents for a week. A race meeting of some distinction was being held some thirty miles away, and Amos was busy with chat of Ugly Duckling being unable to stay the distance and, for his money, the 'Frenchman' had the three thirty in the bag. His money – all 20p of it.

'Ooooh!' squeaked one of the maidens, 'what say we go to the races, Myrt? We never been to the races.'

'Ooooh', let's', squeaked Myrt.

'You two silly kids', pronounced Grandpa from behind his cornerwise pint, 'want your heads tested. You wouldn't know which way to turn on a race course. You'd want somebody to show you the ropes – like my friend Amos, here. Amos,' he called flippantly, 'what about a day at the races to show a pair of hare-brained young fillies that it's a mug's game? Young Myrtle's got her old banger of a car.'

Amos considered the proposition. 'Come to think of it I haven't been on the course this six years or more. Yes', he added, 'I don't mind going along with them termorrer'.

'You don't know what you're letting yourself in for', said Grandpa, and, 'Ooooooh will you *really* Mr Pilling?' twittered Myrtle.

'I said I didn't mind, didn't I? Yes, I'll go along with ye.'

And upon the following morning the unlikely trinity set off, the sisters in figure-hugging pants, Amos wearing collar and tie and 1935-ish brown suit.

It was seven o'clock that evening when Amos and the girls, the latter looking somewhat flushed and fluttery, pushed open the taproom door of *The Star*. 'What's up with you two?' said Grandpa, 'lost your pay packets, I suppose? Well, you'll know better another time now you've learned your lesson.' He paused in a silence broken only by giggles. 'Well?' said Grandpa, 'Go on – say something. Looks to me as though you two've been drowning your sorrows. That it?'

'We only had the one bottle of champagne, Grandad', said Myrt.

'*Champagne?* Champagne, is it? Here', he said in sudden agitation, 'What's all this? What's been going on?'

The girls seemed about to burst through their tight pants with the giggles and squiggles. 'Go on, Mr Pilling', said Tracy, sister to Myrtle, 'Go on, Mr Pilling – you tell him.'

Amos walked slowly to the bar, 'Had a bit o' luck' he said, 'it's drinks all round – I got the Tote Jackpot, that's what.'

'The Jackpot? Go on – you're kidding.'

'Kidding, am I?' said Amos, the great unimpressionable, 'well, if I'm kidding, take a look at this', and he pulled from his inside jacket pocket a wad of ten-pound notes as thick as a paperback. 'There's four hundred and twenty quid there', said Amos, 'and there's another five hundred to come in the post before the end of the week. Nine hundred and twenty quid, that's what the Jackpot paid out to two of us this afternoon. Picked all seven winners, that's what I did. Dead easy, come to think of it – didn't take me more'n a minute to run through the card.'

True enough, no doubt. Seven ticks don't take up much of anybody's time. But which ticks? 'Nine hundred and twenty quid for five bob, that's what I got', said Amos, buying me the first pint which I had consciously had from him in full thirty years!

There can be few pleasures greater than that of beholding great good fortune coming, at the moment, to somebody whom you know well and who could well do with it. Like a forest fire the news crackled round the Parish Pump. Amos Pilling had gone to the races with the two Plockton girls – good for a smile in the first place – got the Tote Jackpot up and won himself nearly a thousand quid. Go on, you're kidding. He's pulling the wool over your eyes. Kidding? Not a bit of it. Go and ask him yourself. I tell you, I've seen pretty well half of it in tenners.

You are expecting me to say that the champagne flowed that night in *The Star and Wheelbarrow*. It did no such thing. Everybody present was asked by Amos what he – or she – would take, and everybody, meeting that calm and cautious eye, took exactly what they might ordinarily have taken – pint of bitter, bottle of Guinness, lager-and-lime! Did Amos say, 'Go on, make it a short?' He did not, for Amos is, was and ever shall be the great unimpressionable whose cap has never been seen to fly over the fence. And was he to alter in his own personal habits? Not he.

Playfully it was suggested that he buy himself a car, a bathroom, a porch, a set of trendy shirts, a fortnight in the Bahamas. The world was his oyster. Amos proposed to leave that oyster unopened. Daily he makes his regular dinnertime call at *The Star and Wheelbarrow*, runs through the runners and riders over precisely one and a half pints, says 'Anybody going through to the bookies? You are, Bert? Well, I'd like a tenpenny win-double *Stewed Prune* and *Bully Boy*.' Has Amos started to bet in pounds? He has not. People, of course, still point him out in hushed whispers, though the teasing grows less and less.

I wouldn't have minded fifty quid of that myself for a nice weekend break in Dieppe. But, after all, who am I to need a weekend's break in a lifetime which is one long holiday?

CHAPTER NINETEEN

IN THE SEASON OF THE YEAR

IT IS OCTOBER again, and the moon which they call the Hunters' Moon falls due shortly to float at the full above Poachers' Wood. Poachers' Wood is not so named without good reason, since it lies, full eight acres of it, so easy of access to the homes of what once were the cottages of the Parish, some ninety per cent of their homesteads 'tied' to the Manor for whose owner they most of them worked.

There is Poachers' Wood, separated only by a single narrow neck of pasture from the rhododendroned frontiers of the formal manorial grounds. It is a mixed wood of beech, wych-elm, oak, ash and sycamore, tapestried with windflowers and bluebells in spring season and richly tenanted by fat pheasants at all times of the year – especially now with the new season's hatchings full plumaged and on the wing – and official sanction to raise the Saturday guns.

Ken Sparrow is gamekeeper to his Lordship of the Manor, a spry old fellow with breeches, brown leather boots and gaiters polished to the perfection of young horse-chestnuts fresh from the velvet cushioning of their protecting husks. Ken wears too a jacket in the Norfolk style, and looks, every inch of him, just what he is – a gamekeeper of the old school. It is not all that long ago since Ken Sparrow abandoned the time-honoured practice of setting his pheasants' eggs under fat brown broody hens, and took to incubation. 'Broodies', it became clear, were not to be found in sufficient quantity to hatch the Manor's requirements for coverts stocked heavily enough to give season-long sport to his Lordship's chosen friends.

Albeit, Ken leaves much nursery work to nature in the wild. 'It stands to reason', he says, 'as birds brought up by their own mothers in the wild is all the wilder, and the sweeter, and gives better sport. Like a babby', he adds, 'is best off at its dam's breast.'

Should one wander about the open coves or inner clearings of Poachers' Wood one may still find Ken's warning gibbets to predators – bedraggled corpses of carrion crows, magpies, squirrels, rats, stoats and weasels fixed with clothes pegs to the wires. Though there is still doubt in my mind as to whether the hungry carrion crow upon the wing is much deterred from his intentions by seeing the shattered plumage of his uncle, or the weasel from his at the sight of the ginger body of his aunt swinging in the breeze.

Ken believes otherwise. 'They varmints', says he, 'thinks twice when they sees what can happen to them if they goes after my young birds'.

Ken plays the trombone in the Steepleborough and District Salvation Army band on Sundays, and wears a different uniform from that of his workaday week. And if ever he were called upon to blow a Last Trump over the body of another predator whom he would not be averse to see hanging from the big oak tree centre of Poachers' Wood it would be to salute the passing of 'Ossie' Badgers in transit for his Satanic eternity.

'Ossie', so called on account of his association with horses as a farrier in World War I, is scarcely ever out of uniform. The King's Khaki of those days was built to last – and last it has in 'Ossie's' case for rising sixty years. His Army boots – three pairs of them – he swears to be as good as new, though tunic, breeches and greatcoat (not always worn together) show signs of wear and tear. He *does* have items of civilian clothing, but there's always a touch of the King's Khaki about 'Ossie' Badgers, and this merges deftly with the turning foliage of autumn days. And nights.

'Ossie's' 'old woman', Mabel Badgers, used once to come to clean our place up once a week. It was on a bright mid-April morning in our first year of residence that she arrived with a small carrier bag containing nine pheasant eggs. 'I thought you might be doing with these', she said, arranging the pretty things on a kitchen plate, 'You'll find they scrambles beautiful.'

'But, Mrs Badgers – no, look here we – I mean – no, we can't. . .'

'I can't see why not', said the lady, 'things being like what they

96

are with this Government. There they was laying under the hedge back of our place, plain enough for anyone to see as got eyes in his head. What's more, my "Ossie" got the thing what sat atop of them. But we're having she.'

She was right. They scrambled beautiful, this clutch of improper fruit. The sweeter for being forbidden, and, as Mrs Badgers had rightly said, 'things being like what they are with this Government'! The texture of the Government, however, would have been – and was – wholly immaterial concerning the matter in hand, or sauce-pan.

'Ossie', aged eighty plus, is I believe the last of those countrymen who sang in their hearts, if not from their throats:

> 'Oh! 'tis my delight on a shiny night
> In the season of the year.'

'I'll have 'e one of these nights again', says Ken Sparrow, eyeing the old enemy innocently homing along the road from *The Star and Wheelbarrow*. 'Mark you my words, I'll have 'e again.'

A couple of years ago 'Ossie', good citizen that he is, went for renewal of his gun licence at the Police Station in Steepleborough.

'Any convictions?' asked the Sergeant good naturedly, eyeing the old warrior with something approaching affection.

'Convictions?' said 'Ossie', 'What sort of convictions was ye thinking about? I never had no convictions. No, wait, I'm a liar. I had one of they, must be all of twenty five years ago. That Ken Sparrow come at me one night in the little old wood. Well, and what if I did have me gun with me? That didn't prove nothing, did it? I'd me right to carry a fire-arm, hadn't I? Ye never know what might come at ye of a night-time these days. And what if Ken Sparrow *had* picked up a little old hen bird still warm? Didn't mean as I'd shot it, did it? I wasn't the only one as was up in the wood that night, I can tell ye. But 'e 'ad *me* all right.'

'Well, don't let him catch you again, that's all', said the Sergeant.

'What, me going out of a night-time at my time o' life?' said 'Ossie', 'I got better things to do.'

He hasn't though, and well Ken Sparrow knows it. But he knows, and we know, and 'Ossie' knows that his Lordship of the Manor takes a kindly view of the old man's delight of a shiny night. Ken may, indeed, 'have 'e' again, but his Lordship, faced with his fulminating gamekeeper, will take no action. 'Ossie' Badgers can't do that much harm, and the old fellow, reasons his Lordship, hasn't got all those pleasures left to him in life.

The whole world loves a poacher, saving a gamekeeper—though not the organised poaching gangs which have been known to descend from heaven knows where upon Poachers' Wood. It's the traditional loner pitting his wits and country lore against authority who commands affection. Like young Ron Oates who lived once around our Parish Pump and was the craftiest collector of 'long-tailed 'uns' for many a mile around.

Once, after he'd 'delivered the bread' – for he was a baker's roundsman – at our kitchen door, my wife discovered that one of the loaves had feathers on it. 'Ron', she said, 'would you – could you – take me poaching with you one night? Really, I mean it.'

'Look, missus', said Ron, 'I couldn't do a thing like that. What'd the village say if Ken caught us?'

Ah, what, indeed! My wife said – and truthfully – that she was writing a book and that poaching came into the story. She wanted it to be authentic. No, she promised the anxious Ron, his name would neither appear in the book nor the escapade mentioned to a living soul in the village. And certainly not at Sunday morning's cocktail party at the Manor!

'Well' said Ron, 'If you're game I'm on. It's up to you, mind you. I like a bit of sport about a woman, and that's the truth. Come back of my place nine o'clock time Tuesday. Moon's on the way out.'

I started on at her with the 'For God's sake, darling' stuff, but that was no good. Wearing black slacks and a navy duffle coat she set off over the fields for the back of Ron's place.

It was near midnight when she came slinking through our back-door, bird in hand. 'There', she said, 'Oh, but it was the thrill of my life.'

'Well', I heard myself yapping, 'What happened? How did he do it?'

'Do you think I'd tell you that?' said my wife, 'That's my business – and Ron's. No, don't worry, I'll not go again.'

Her eyes wore an expression inscrutable and dreamlike. He was a lithe and handsome young fellow, was Ron Oates. A pretty woman, my wife. Come, come, such thoughts would never do. She'd just gone poaching, that was all, so I left it at that!

CHAPTER TWENTY

THATCHING MEN

FOR THE PAST week or two the thatchers have been busy with the roof of the cottage called 'Swales' which stands upon the green at no great distance from the Parish Pump. 'Swales'? Queer sort of name for a cottage. Why 'Swales'? What does it mean? I will tell you. It is so named after an elephantine, bombazined lady with a high collar and a toupee who once resided there. Miss Agatha Swale ran the left hand of her two front rooms as – well, you'd hardly call it a shop, since its resources were so slim. Tall jars of sweets, toffee apples in season, sherbet dabs, assorted biscuits, shag tobacco, Wild Woodbines, liquorice allsorts and suchlike. None of the heavy duty stuff of grocery such as ham, bacon or even cheese. There was once, I was told, a glassed Paysandu Tongue on the shelf, but for which there were no takers over some three years. It finally vanished, maybe into the deep gorge of Agatha Swale herself.

'Swale's Shop', that's what the little place was called. Or more usually plain 'Swales'. Those who bought the cottage shortly after the departure of Agatha Swale for some such place as human elephants go to die, were bold enough as to rename the property 'Little Thatch'. They might have named it 'The Limes' for all the village cared. 'Swales' was 'Swales' was 'Swales'. The successors of those first purchasers had the good sense and feeling to give in and restore to their home the name by which it had for all of thirtyfive years been known about the Parish Pump. 'Swales'.

'We allus called it "Swales",' said the ancient men in *The Star and Wheelbarrow*, 'so the new folks is right enough. "Swales", that's what its name is. But I tell ye, us kids wasn't half skeered of old Agatha Swale. Not a ha'porth o' tick'd she give ye. Shout ye out of the shop, she would.'

Miss Agatha Swale was in the last few months of her occupancy when first I came to the village to live some fifty yards away, and, like Agatha Swale, right opposite the long now demolished village school. Her emporium was designed to serve the school kids with aniseed balls and such at sixteen a penny, and pensioners for fags and shag. She was well positioned for the school kids, both before and after school, and the pensioners on passage to and from the allotments had to pass her door.

I can see her well in the eye of memory, all jet, bombazine and cameo brooches, a Goliath of a lady whose top hamper towered above the counter. 'Got no call for it, Mister', she said, pleasantly enough, when I ventured to seek marmalade of her on one occasion, 'Folks around these parts eats jam.'

Fly-papers encrusted with sorrowfully waving legs hung from the ceiling and bluebottles buzzed about her windowpanes until she deemed there to be sufficient numbers of them to swat the lot. Had there been such a thing as a Food Inspector in those casually low and far off times he would have been given short shrift from Agatha Swale. 'Just you keep your poking nose out of my business', she would have declared from all her majesty of height and depth, length and breadth. 'Go on, be off with you. Clear out of my shop, or I'll call the Police.'

It was seeing the thatchers on the roof of 'Swales' that recalled Agatha to mind. And, come to think of it, her fat cat Sam, who sat all day upon the counter staring balefully at the customers with moonlight eyes. A Food Inspector would have had something to say about Sam sitting there among the open cardboard boxes of allsorts, jelly beans and jelly babies.

The thatchers of today are a pair of sinewy young fellows, strangers from another county, who come daily in a little blue van laden mostly, it would appear, with thermos flasks and slabs of sandwiches. They do not darken the dinnertime doors of the *Star and Wheelbarrow*. They are the new style craftsmen, hard working, expensive, silent and impersonal. No dinnertime pints and badinage for these, vividly contrasting with the so-called working habit of Ben Sanders (retired), last of the old school of local thatchers living on the outskirts of market town Steepleborough with a five mile radius of villages as his territory. Let it be proclaimed that Ben

Sanders was independent, bone idle and a boozer to boot. He punctuated his passing – by bicycle, by pints in pubs. Ten o'clock opening time at the Bilberry *Green Man*, ten forty five, and with two miles behind him, a thirst-quencher in *The Dragon* at Little Sleeping. Another mile, and *The Half Moon* at the cross-roads would claim his attention. 'Well', he would say in there, 'this'll never do. Time I was at wuk.' If a roof in our village was his destination, then he felt it only courteous to take a quick half in *The Star* to give him heart for the task ahead. Noon was his E.T.A. at any given site, and at one o'clock it was time to knock off for dinner which accompanied him in a small wooden box tied with twine to the carrier of his bicycle. This, were he at our end, would naturally enough be consumed in *The Star and Wheelbarrow* which, with marked reluctance, he would leave at two thirty closing time.

In summertime Ben would sometimes manage a five hour day. In the winter months the customer for his services would be lucky to have him three hours aloft. Withal, he contrived to be a craftsman of distinction, and his steady balance at ladder-top could evoke nothing but astonished respect.

He met his match with tough old Miss Parkinson of 'Pear Tree Cottage'. 'Mr Sanders', she said, 'I require a precise estimate of the cost to me of materials and your hourly time-rate for the job. I expect you to be here not later than ten o'clock in the morning. You may take your dinner on *my* premises, and I will provide you with a pint of light ale to go with it. You will *not*, while working for me, go to the village inn. What is more, I will pay you weekly, and by the hour, and *not* a lump sum for the job.'

So stunned was Ben by this approach, and so attracted by the notion of cash on every Friday for a trouble-free weekend, that after a first feeble, 'Now, you listen to me ma'am. . .' he accepted the terms.

Gazing, as I have been doing from time to time, at the brisk young fellows on the roof-tree of 'Swales', I think of Ben Sanders, the idle old toper on his wavering bicycle. But I think with greater esteem and affection of Henry Stobbs, resident thatcher of this very Parish when first I came to live in it over thirty years ago. Henry Stobbs with leather knee-pads over his corduroys, a steel-blue eye, a huge moustache, and a brass stud in his uncollared shirt was a master craftsman. Slowly rhythmical in his work with straw truss, mallet and sprindle pegs which he cut upon the site with the same razor-edged clasp knife with which he clove the crusty bread and slab of cheese which served him for elevenses. To watch him upon a roofside – pronounced 'ruff' in these parts – was to behold the perfection of unhurried coordination of mind, muscle and eye.

I had been in residence no more than a couple of months when, upon a grey December afternoon, my answer to the door knocker revealed Henry Stobbs standing without.

'Good afternoon, Mr Stobbs', said I, 'and what can I do for you?'

'Arternoon, master', replied Henry Stobbs, 'It's what I'm going to do for ye as I stopped by to tell ye. I'll be starting on that ruff o' yourn come March.'

'But, Mr Stobbs, I . . .'

Nor had I even thought about, leave alone budgeted for, a rethatch 'come March'. Oh, it was a bit rough here and there, but could surely go another two to three years without attention. And I said so.

'That's what you may think, master', said Henry Stobbs, 'but I'm telling ye as three years from now and we'll have to fetch the whole of 'e off to the ridge. Come March, and I'll fetch off the half of 'e and re-ruff all over to the weather. Wants doing come March. Arternoon to ye, master.'

I stammered something about maybe not being able to afford the service when the time came.

'Ye don't want to go bothering yerself that way', said Henry Stobbs, 'Ye can pay me when ye feels as ye can. But that ruff o' yourn's got to be done.'

What's more, it was 'come March' as Henry Stobbs, master of his craft, had so declared. Every straw-covered 'ruff' in the Parish was his personal care and concern. A ragged 'ruff' anywhere in his patch was more than he could bear to see.

I had the immense good fortune to place an old-fashioned twenty shillings upon the long-priced winner of the Two thousand Guineas that spring and to double it up with the winner of the One thousand.

'Mind ye, I wasn't worried about the money, master', said Henry as I handed over the crisp cash, 'It could've waited a twelvemonth for all as I cared. All the ruffs in this place has to look right, and that's the end o' it. And the wire'll keep the little old starlings off of their burrowings.'

The lithe young thatching men from the next county are doing all right, and wiring over the fancy ridge they've fashioned with great expertise. Just in time, too, for the wintering starlings from Scandinavia are already swathing the sunsets of November with scarves of spectacular flight. The young men are fine – but they're neither of them a Henry Stobbs. And that's a fact.

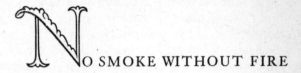

CHAPTER TWENTY-ONE

NO SMOKE WITHOUT FIRE

THERE HAVE BEEN a great many snide things, both in poetry and prose, written about the month of November. Thomas Hood, I suppose, took the heartiest side-swipe of them all with his:

'No warmth, no cheerfulness, no healthful ease,
    No comfortable feel in any member –
No shade, no shine, no butterflies, no bees,
No fruits, no flowers, no leaves, no birds,
        November!'

He was a bit adrift about the birds. Starlings in whirling scarves of flight pass over the surly sundowns of the month; titmice hang by their heels from bacon rind in gardens; the Parish is bustling with bullfinches about last fragments of honeysuckle berries, and fieldfares chack-chack about the tattered remnants of the pink fruit of the yews. Lapwings on the ploughland, rooks in the evening elms, a dramatic passage of waxwings through the conifers, storm-cocks yelling from treetops against navy-blue storm clouds of north-westerlies, finches in the hedgerows, and, aggressively eternal by every back door, the Christmas-card robin.

No true dearth of birds, Mr Hood, but maybe you're right about the flowers, save the cold yellow opening of winter jasmine against house walls and last forlorn, unpicked chrysanthemums like grubby dish-rags at the farthest end of the November garden.

For her own immaculately faint praise of November give me this from Jane Austen's Journal:

'What fine weather this is! Not very becoming perhaps early

in the morning, but very pleasant out of doors at noon, and very wholesome – at least everybody fancies so, and imagination is everything.'

Local imagination has risen traumatically over past weeks at the thought of the open and dewy pastureland behind Fulmer's Farm being turned into a featureless complex of little boxes, all made of ticky-tacky. Thirty of them. How slyly, it seems, the Executors of the Estate of Frederick Fulmer, deceased, set about their scheme to have bungalows rather than beasts on the pasture. They sought, it appears, planning permission from the R.D.C., to bring about what is picturesquely called 'In-Filling.' Ribbon development we have long known to be 'out'. but 'In-Filling' within the perimeter of the Parish Boundary is a different matter. And the R.D.C. has looked with discreet benevolence on the building of the odd little house here, the couple of bungalows there. But *thirty!* This was a very different matter.

'They tell me', said some young fellow from an adjacent Parish, 'that you're going to have a housing estate hereabouts.'

The scene was the Saloon Bar of the *Star and Wheelbarrow* around the lunchtime hour. Miss Grisby of 'Wistarias' was in there sipping a pre-prandial glass of sherry wine, and leafing through a rose catalogue.

'I beg your pardon, young man', she said, 'You said *what?*'

'I aid that they're talking about a housing estate – thirty new houses.'

Miss Grisby perceptibly paled. Her voice rose by many decibels. '*Housing estate?*' she spurted, '*What* housing estate? *Thirty* houses? Where? When?'

'Of course, it's only something I heard. I may be quite wrong. You know how these rumours get around. But I *did* hear that it was to be on the land back of Fulmer's Farm.'

'At the back of *Fulmer's Farm?* I just *don't* believe it. Jessie Fulmer wouldn't dream of doing anything so dreadful. Why, Fred Fulmer would turn in his grave.'

'He was cremated, wasn't he?' said some local joker.

'Well, well – whatever. Oh, no, Jessie would *never* do a thing like that to us. It would be sheer vandalism – *sheer* vandalism. I just don't believe a word of it.'

It has to be said that there is no smoke without fire, and it has to be added that nothing raises the blood pressure of the rural

community more rapidly than talk of property prices and development. Interest is instant, 'bush telegraphs' hum like bees from
hedgetop to hedgetop. The long ago top priority titbit that some
nubile maiden was no better than she should be and had deservedly
got herself into trouble is way down bottom of the pops today.
'Planning Permission' is the goblin at the bottom of our gardens,
and Jessie Fulmer not only *dreamed* of 'doing a thing like that', but
jolly well did it. She planned to go and live in Malta and she could
do with the cash.

But – and there is ever a but. 'There!' cried Miss Grisby some
weeks later, triumphantly waving the local Weekly to all in the
Star and Wheelbarrow. 'There. The R.D.C. have turned it down flat.
Now we can sleep easy in our beds.'

That, of course, is where she is wrong. Parish Councils may pass
mumbling resolutions to Rural District Councils, and Rural
District Councils can refuse sanction allegedly to despoil out of
hand. But above all, like some great albatross of omen, there soars
the County – faceless foes when they seem not to be upon our
personal side, friends in high places when they're 'one of us'.

Jessie Fulmer has not taken the high-handed 'no' of the R.D.C.
lying down. Oh, dear me, no! She has gone over their heads to the
County. Notice of Appeal has been lodged. And, while the County
investigates and cogitates, Miss Grisby may not yet sleep easy in
her bed. And nor, of course, may Jessie Fulmer.

We who have the good fortune to live around Parish Pumps, even
in sour days of November, lead lives so filled with events of seemingly unimportant importancies that there is no time to be bored.
Local happenings touch upon us with an immediate and personal
impact. We are more deeply stirred by the pending arrival of thirty
free range chickens in the meadow over the road this afternoon than
by the hypothetical cost of eggs in the Common Market.

As a matter of fact the free range chickens *have* arrived, and the
whole Parish is loud in its applause. Come to think of it, we've
hardly seen a Buff Orpington, a Rhode Island or a White Wyandotte
for years. Nor heard cock-crow other than that from the end of Nut
Lane where, twice each year, the two gypsy families encamp
during the pea picking and potato-lifting seasons, bringing their
dozen or so fowls with them. So chickens compel our interest, as
well as speculation as to what those men from the Water Board
think they're doing prodding with long poles into the bed of the

brook. How strange that Sam and Ada Gilderson proudly refuse to take part in any of the browsings and sluicings, the coach trips and kindred genial amenities organised by, and for, the Over-Sixties Club! Is it true – as they say – that *The Bay Horse* at Gosling Green is changing hands and has been bought from the Brewery as a Free House for £35,000?

'£35,000? You're joking. For that dump?'

'That's what I heard.'

'Who's got that kind of money?'

'Somebody said it's a syndicate that's bought it. And if the new road comes. . .'

'New road? That'll be the day. I'll believe that when I see it, and the same goes for main drainage, *and* street lighting. . .'

May the Lord in His infinite Mercy protect us from street lighting and keep The Valley Green Stores plentifully supplied with a full range of torch batteries. They're prone to forget about this until November catches up with them.

But by and large let rumour – benevolent rumour – run rife around the Parish Pump. When, many years ago, I moved temporarily a very short distance from one parish to another into a little house hard by their village pub, I was asked some months later: 'How are you and your wife getting on with your pub in Much Middling?'

'My pub in *Much Middling?*'

'Yes, somebody told me you'd taken this pub in Much Middling and your wife was doing super meals.'

This didn't take much working out. We had rented a cottage *next* to a pub in this village also beginning with the letter 'M'. My wife had once said at a party that she'd love to go in for catering! So there we were in our Much Middling tavern at the drop of a hat.

Rumours? Great. Who is the handsome and casually groomed middle-aged man who has just bought – for £18,500 someone said – the little residence over the hill called Brick Cottage? He has a sports car, *and* a rather swagger motor bicycle. Unusual sort of chap. Someone says he's a television actor, others that he's a well-known amateur yachtsman. We'll have to ask the blighter round for a drink and find out!

CHAPTER TWENTY-TWO

THE HUSH OF THE GREY SEASON

IT IS NOVEMBER, and it is no use pretending any more that it isn't. The beech leaves drift into the sodden grass by the bend in the brook where the wagtails nested, and tattered foliage of wych-elm has made a shallow counterpane around that still-standing finger-post of yesterday, the Parish Pump. The chacking fieldfares have all but polished off the juicy pink berries of the yew tree by the Post Office, and the finches, like clockwork toys, flock voicelessly in the hedgerows. Cock pheasants crow in misty dusk of dawn and evening, and the lengthening nights are looped with the hollow music of the hunting owls. Wrote Thomas Hood:

No Sunday newspapers this weekend either!

It was earlier in the autumn when, as kettles had boiled for early morning tea, two cups of it drunk and the table laid for breakfast, that a sense of something not quite right made itself felt around the Parish Pump. By nine fifteen at the very latest we should have heard the little van pull up mid-village and listened for the footsteps of Perce in one direction and Fred in the other proclaiming the arrival of the weekly drug of the Sabbath – the 'Sundays'. All about it – Giles, Tottenham, missing schoolgirl, John ('he doth protest too much') Junor, snide television, theatre and film criticism, Monastic Turkish Caves in joyous supplementary colour, the Love Life of Genghis Khan, amusing Miss Whitehorn, depressing Cross Bencher, 'British Athlete on Drug Charge', 'Was Waterloo Worth It?', Bikini Time in the Lacadive Islands – all the gozzy gallimaufrey of culture-vulturism and philistinism which make a kind of harmless 'fix' of Sunday mornings.

No throb of the little van in the village street, no Perce, no Fred, no papers. A strike? No, there had been no talk of a strike. A train derailment? Surely not. Fred and Perce upside down in a ditch? A possibility, we supposed. Or they were just, for good reason of their own, lazy and late on this particular Sunday? The empty abyss deepened. The church bells began, with melancholy compulsion, to proclaim a more fitting way to spend the hour from eleven to twelve than that of deciding whether the late Miss Marilyn Munro was schizophrenic, paranoic, or plain manic-depressive.

A telephone call. It was Miss Patterson from her outlying cottage, 'Hazelnuts'. 'Oh – I just telephoned to wonder – I hope I haven't woken you up – but have your Sunday papers arrived? I haven't had *mine*.'

'No, Miss Patterson, ours haven't arrived, either. I don't think anybody's have. No sign of the van in the village.'

'Oh, dear! What *can* have happened to them?'

'Clearly, there's been some kind of a hold-up, Miss Patterson.'

'Oh, well, I suppose we shall just have to wait and see – but somehow, Sunday morning without the papers. . .'

Yes, indeed, drowsy drug addicts that we be, Sunday morning without the papers . . .! A yawning gap. Nail-biting, curtain-twitching, room-pacing. All very well for the remote snobberies of those who wouldn't be seen dead with Sunday paper rubbish, anyway. The most of us were – are – unashamedly trembling at the knees with human weakness, and a healthy hour's worship or digging in the garden are no substitute for 'Life or Death in my Surgery' by A Doctor.

An air of the deepest despondency breathed through both Tap Room and Saloon Bar of *The Star and Wheelbarrow* at five past twelve. It deepened as customers densened towards twelve thirty. 'Anybody had their papers yet?' 'We haven't got ours.' 'Anyone thought of ringing up Steepleborough?' 'Seems all funny, somehow – Sunday without the papers.'

It wasn't funny at all.

'Oh, Lord', said one of the bright young men of the Parish, gazing out of the window. 'Not the Fuzz!'

'The Fuzz?'

'Yes – call them the Cops, if you like. What do *they* want?'

True enough, the 'Fuzz' it was in the uniformed person of our own P.C. Furrow, stepping briskly from his little blue-lettered

Police van and shoving his head around the Tap Room door.

'Anybody want any papers?' said P.C. Furrow. 'I was just coming off duty at Steepleborough – stopped at the newsagents, and Gwen there said that Perce and Fred had handed in their notice. Well, I thought – no harm in keeping the peace by putting a dozen or two "sale-or-returns" back of the car. Mind you, I suppose I shouldn't be doing this, but as I'm on the way home, anyway. . .'

In an instant the 'Fuzz' had his image changed from Public Persecutor to Public Benefactor. Uproar was instant and heart-warming. Sudden sunshine gleamed through the murk of the paperless morning. Constable Furrow had chosen his selection with – though not for him, you understand – commercial foresight. The three publications on offer were those certain of acceptance by audiences of Radio's 1 and 2 and ITV. The egg-headed minority – *Times, Observer, Telegraph* – could take *Sunday People, Sunday Mirror, News of the World*, or else. . .'

Gratefully I grabbed a pair, and full-bosomed casements, could such things be, opened on seas far from perilous or forlorn.

May I say that the following Sunday, slacks and pullover above pyjamas, I rode myself into Steepleborough after first tea break, and bought my usuals. An hour later P.C. Furrow turned up outside the cottage. 'I brought your high-brow one this week', he said, 'and the other.' Alas for his kindness, but I had already done so. 'Never mind', said he, 'I'll get rid of the posh one to somebody.' And he did, to an elderly man of letters who later drifted, all paperless, into *The Star*. The 'posh one' was, as it happened, the one not usually taken by my neighbour. But, squinting through his bifocals and rather down his nose at it, he was duly grateful. 'I've often wondered what that rag was all about', he said.

Now, with still no deliveries, the Sunday paper crisis has entered a climate of somewhat confused neighbourliness. 'If you *do* happen to be going in tomorrow. . .?' 'Well, actually, John Stairway's going in, and he's getting *mine*.' 'Oh, do you think he'd get *mine*?' 'Better ring him up, hadn't you, and ask him? Oh, no, come to think of it he said he was going out to dinner tonight.' 'Oh, dear, then I'd better go in myself – anybody want a paper if I go in. . .?'

There is some undecisive thinking about drawing up a rota, but it will come to nothing. Before long a new paid-up little van will come throbbing down the street again, and we will all be able to sleep long and easy in our Saturday night beds!

If we have been missing our newspapers of a Sunday, we have been missing our 'strangers' too, mostly over weekends, but on week days, too. 'Strangers?' Yes, the passing holidaymakers of summertime, the fine weather weekend wanderers. People in luggage-packed Estate cars crawling with Crisp-munching, Coke sucking kids, Germans with cameras, Swedes with spectacles, citizens of the United States rootling around the churchyard for ancestors, young couples in very new Spitfires or very old Minis. Come September's end and they are down to a trickle: come November and, house guests apart, they have vanished.

Apart from one stranger who awoke me from brief summer siesta by poking his camera lens against the sitting-room window to take a madly clever picture of garden viewed via domestic interior (with me in wing chair) and French doors beyond, practically all passers-by have been viewed either passing by, stacking up with ice creams in the Post Office or casing *The Star and Wheelbarrow* from without and debating as to which door to enter – Public Bar, or Saloon.

And by whichever door they do – or did – decide to enter they would be greeted, poor devils, by that inevitable hush in conversation among the natives. Watch it, chaps – strangers about. It is not that we are prone to be cold and unfriendly to our visitors, only that, as with every rural community, the stranger must be viewed with reserve and a measure of suspicion. What the devil is *he* doing here, that fat man with bushy whiskers, gold rimmed spectacles and sky-blue pants? Who on earth are *these*, the blue-rinse lady in the twinset and the balding man in lightweight suit?

'What will you have, dear?'

'A gin and tonic, please, dear.'

'That's a gin and tonic, please – *with* ice and lemon if you've got them – oh, you have – good. That's a gin and tonic, then, and a pint of bitter. Oh, er, and – do you do sandwiches?'

Of course we do sandwiches, you condescending fat-head. What do you think we are – a bunch of bumpkins living in the last century? Can't you read the notice on the bar? Snacks and Sandwiches, it says. Yes, it *is* a pretty village, isn't it? At least we think so. Glad you like it. Have you come far? Oh, from the other side of Watford, have you? Yes, I suppose you are getting rather built up. Yes, I suppose we *are* lucky. How far to Peterborough – to *Peterborough?*

'John, how far do you reckon to Peterborough from here?'

'Peterborough? Never really thought about it. I suppose – let me think – I suppose if you go by Huntingdon about, say, fifty miles?'

'My dear John, you don't have to *touch* Huntingdon – you must be out of your mind. I'd say, sir, if you go by way of Cambridge – good fast road – it'd be forty to forty five miles from where we are. Somewhere nice to stay near there? Sorry, but there you have me.'

We ourselves, of course, have been 'strangers' in taverns about Parish Pumps other than our own, seeking direction, seeking sandwiches, fighting through the daunting fog of native 'hush' which descends upon our entry. Neither the natives of those parts, nor we of ours, go quite as far as the old *Punch* comment on the English character – 'Look, there's a furriner – 'eave 'alf a brick at 'im.'

But there remains the disturbing first reaction in the subconscious that strangers can't be up to any good. Though, happily enough, *rapport* soon arrives with the right kind, whereupon we become, if not chauvinistic, at least heartily proud of our *ambience* and eager to show what warm-hearted, helpful and hospitable folk we are.

'Drop in again next time you're passing.'

'We will – we certainly will. It's been great meeting you.'

'It's been nice meeting *you* – have a good trip.'

'We will – *we* will. . . And thanks for your help.'

Truth to tell, we rather miss the shot in the arm which the passing stranger bestows, although still to be viewed with dis-relish are any two young men with theodolites going about whatever is their mysterious business, and any person seen to be carrying a clipboard!

As Nathan, from his corner-by-right in *The Star*, will say: 'There's no telling what them sort's getting up to, and that's a fact.'

It is – even though a shade negative!

Now the homely hush of the grey season descends, and the community, quite gratefully, sinks back upon itself. The lion-gold hustle of harvest is long gone, and the potatoes are lifted. The inhospitable, if customer-caring, sign 'NO PEAPICKERS' has long vanished from the doors of *The Star and Wheelbarrow* and, as usual, a blind eye was turned to it by anyone officially concerned with the field of 'discrimination'. Fêtes, gymkhanas, carnivals, steam-traction rallies and cricket on the green are departed, likewise the savage in-fighting of the Fruit, Flower and Vegetable show. Christmas pends, and for a full week there has been a vehicle lettered 'Rapier Brothers. Domestic Heating Service'. Looks as though the Wedgewoods are going in for 'oil-fired'. Bert Thicket reported seeing a king-sized storage tank being carried round the back. Hmmm! The Wedgewoods must have had a windfall – or something worth talking about!

It is passing peaceful – 'no fruits, no flowers, no leaves, no birds – November.' Even though the 'no birds' bit is not all that true. The starlings at sundown whirl in rushing scarves across the sky, rooks trail homeward, tits tap on milk bottle tops and window panes, and the backdoor robin regards his territory through possessive round eyes, glossy as blackberries.

CHAPTER TWENTY-THREE

SHOULD AULD ACQUAINTANCE..?

ONCE UPON A very long time ago – 1945 to be precise – we had a soldier for the New Year. That is to say, for the last night of the Old Year and the first night of the New. To be exact we had one genuine soldier, a private in the Argyll and Sutherland Highlanders, and one languid layabout attired in the wingless tunic of an R.A.F. uniform, grey flannel trousers, brown brogues and an R.A.F. greatcoat.

London friends of ours who were to be house guests for a day or two had found this ill-assorted pair at eight o'clock in the evening standing on the gale-swept platform of our shelterless railway junction. They were not only lost, but liquored, and penniless to boot.

The languid layabout, in a lisping drawl, explained that he had thought himself in transit for Peterborough, where he had been invited to spend a week's leave with an immoderately wealthy aunt who was a Vanderbilt from New York married to the head of an English Merchant Bank. Our friends thought Peterborough to be an unlikely place of residence for a Merchant Banker, but simply said, oh! they saw. During the morning the Argyll and Sutherlander had been en route for a midday train to Glasgow and Hogmanay when, in some tavern or other, he had fallen in with who he described as 'this daft Pole'.

Clearly, though temporary brothers-in-the-bottle, neither had been able to understand very much of what the other was saying. The Glasgow train had gone by default, though the Highlander produced a travel voucher as evidence of good intention. The 'daft Pole' had somehow explained that *he* was destined for Peter-borough, where the Scottish Soldier could, doubtless, change trains for Edinburgh and travel then to Glasgow. They had better, said the 'daft Pole', string along together. They strung, or clung, together at some afternoon drinking club, took a taxi for the wrong station and here they were.

The languid layabout had imagined that he might change at Cambridge for Peterborough – a likely tale! Both he and the Scottish Soldier fancying our junction to be Cambridge had detrained. And there they were, dramatically destitute and with nowhere to lay their heads upon New Year's Eve of all eves.

Our friends, knowing us to be kindly people, said that they were sure that the orphans of the storm could be offered a night's shelter, if only on the floor. They telephoned us, and we said oh, yes, let them come.

'Fraffly kaind of you' said the man in the wingless tunic, the flannel trousers and the brown brogues. 'Fraffly embarrassing, the whole business. Ai seem to have lost mai wallet. Pickpockets about. Naice place you have here.' He licked his lips at the scent of a goose which was browning in the oven. He sank into an armchair near the fire. 'Fraffly kaind', he said again, 'Ai'm afraid our cousin from over the Border is a traifle haigh.'

Our cousin from over the Border was standing in the kitchen in numb silence, twisting his Balmoral bonnet from hand to hand. Then: 'Ah couldnae help it, ah couldnae help it', he muttered, 'It's yon daft Pole. Ah'd best get awa'. . .'

Neither of them now was clearly 'quaite as haigh' as he had been earlier in the evening. We bade the Scottish Soldier be at ease. He could 'get awa' ' come the morning. Meantime let him consider himself our guest.

'It's sae guid o' ye', he kept saying, 'tae fash yerselves wi' the like o' me.'

We would rather, of course, be fashing ourselves with the likes of him than with the likes of the other.

There was, of course, a war on, *and* it was New Year's Eve, so a visit to *The Star and Wheelbarrow* was suggested, a notion heartily greeted by the wingless wonder, and dourly, haplessly accepted by his companion. The regulars in *The Star* stared in some astonish-ment at our bizarre company, but one of the ancient men, as was the custom in those days, pushed his tankard towards the strangers, saying 'Ye'll tek a sup along o' me, master.'

I will say for our languid guest that he was a quick thinker. Quick to take note of the name of the brewery under whose flag *The Star* then did its business. Quick he was to say, what a coincidence that an uncle of his was Managing Director of that brewery, and that uncle would make everything doubly right with the landlord could sanction be given for his nephew to stand drinks all round to his new-found friends. He had not only had his wallet pinched, he said, but he seemed to have mislaid his cheque book as well. It was all 'Fraffly embarrassing.'

A veil may as well be drawn over the remainder of that memorable New Year's Eve by that Parish Pump of long ago. We ourselves indeed recollect it only as though seen through a glass darkly – or misted over with the glasses of good cheer. Old slyboots stood at attention as Big Ben boomed the entry of 1945, then raised his glass and cried: 'The King, God bless him.'

'Here's tae us', mumbled the Scottish Soldier, adding: 'Are ye nae awa' first footin' one o' ye?'

Came the morn, and with three of our pounds in his pocket the Scottish Soldier took taxi for the station with dreams of Euston and Glasgow shining through the mist of his bewildered eyes. The three pounds – Scottish pound notes! – came through the letter-box four days later.

The wingless wonder spent New Year's Day drinking deep of that bitter beer of whose brewery his uncle was Managing Director. It was on the morning following that, almost by brute force, we shoved him into a taxi with a fiver to help him reach his Vanderbilt aunt in Peterborough. He pinched one of my favourite shirts and we never, of course, heard of him again or saw him again. We squared things up with the *Star and Wheelbarrow* whose then landlord confided in me that he thought there was something fishy about our guest and his Brewery Boss uncle. We were prone to agree.

Other Eves and Days of New Year come to mind as I think back to years spent about this Parish Pump. The first New Year's Eve of all of which mention has been made before. Moving in night, bed in *The Star*, whisky with next-door Scottish neighbours, curtain-up to life around the Parish Pump. And another New Year's Day which followed half a night of still, blanketing fog. The temperature fell dramatically in the night, and with first light came the sun in a pale blue sky floodlighting a frozen village in which, one felt, a *troika* might come jingling through, followed by wolves! No wind blew. All trees, hedges and grass-blades were part of the décor of a temple of ice. Never ever was there a winter's morning of such indescribable beauty as that one. There was a kestrel perched upon the garden gate, and why did the kestrel not move, that 'Windover' of Gerard Manley Hopkins:

'I caught this morning's minion, kingdom of daylight's
    dauphin, dapple-dawn-drawn Falcon, in his riding
Of the rolling level underneath him steady air, and striding
High there...'

Why did not this sunlit kestrel in the archways of blue sky and glittering frost take wing, ride there, stride there, high there? The hawk did take wing, floundered from the gate-post and fell to ground on the turf of the lawn. The bird beautiful could not stride that sky of New Year's Day because the talons, misted over from the eve before, were bound fast together in a lozenge of solid ice.

As I drew near the hawk, fierce of eye, rose lumbering from the ground and somehow carried the deadweight of those frozen claws over the boundary hedge and into the spinney behind the village hall.

That was a New Year's Day for the remembering. And, to set alongside it, a savage night of December 31 when the north-easterly had all day hurled the hard grit of blizzard snow across the landscape. There were parties being held in other villages and hamlets, and to one of these we had been bidden. Walls of snow blocked all three outlets from our hollow by the Parish Pump. Electricity failed, and the village, Wellington-booted, and by torch and hurricane lamp, found its way to the *Star and Wheelbarrow* where paraffin lamplight and candlepower glowed about the yellow fangs of the old pub piano. 'Daisy, Daisy. . .' clattered the piano wires, and 'My old man said follow the van. . .', and 'I've got a motto, always merry and bright. . .' We Auld Lang Syned it at midnight, and never did an old year go out more joyfully, and a new one enter in, than on that Arctic night of nineteen-whatever-it-was.

And now again it is January in the village. The lights of the Twelve Days of Christmas have been dowsed, and the joybells in the church tower are silent – silent as the ancient men of a weekday dinnertime in the tap-room of *The Star and Wheelbarrow* public house.

CHAPTER TWENTY-FOUR

CAREFREE COMPANIONSHIP

ALL OF A sudden it looks unbelievably bleak after Twelfth Night, with the Christmas tree which sparkled in the bay window of *The Star and Wheelbarrow* reduced to ashes at the back of the yard, and only a new 'girlie' calendar to remind us that a New Year has started and that 'girlies', old or new, are for ever.

Of course, in the local town the January Sales have started up, but they are not wildly provident of excitement. One tends to stare at these faked-up-looking price reduction cards with lack-lustre eyes. Even the big spenders would seem to have spent them-selves to a standstill. Things in the Poultry Market, so juicy a short while back with geese and gobblers, are a bit skinny too. The jolly Santa wishing us all a Merry Christmas strikes a sour note above the wired chicken and rabbit cages. The Market Manager has never been known to remove jolly Santa before the beginning of February.

The truth of the matter around the Parish Pump is that the young Clackmannans have gone ski-ing, the Stark family are still recovering from their all-in Christmas five-day package at Margate, old Nathan hasn't budged from his corner in '*The Star*' and that it is always 'January Sales' time in The Post Office Stores.

It is the large cork board hanging left of the Post Office counter which proclaims upon hand-written cards and scraps of paper the sundry requirements of the Rural District, be its residents selling, buying, hiring or seeking hire of their talents – or accommodation. Or, indeed, seeking accommodation itself. The drawingpin-pitted Post Office board is an unceasing revelation of the beating heart of the Parish, employment exchange, car mart, rent office, junk shop, outfitters' all in one.

'Leotard, scarcely used, dry cleaned, excellent condition, 75p.'

Presumably the lady at the back of that telephone number is herself in excellent condition after half a dozen keep fit classes, or just as fair, fat and forty as ever, having found the whole thing a bit of a drag. There's something a shade erotic in the thought of ringing the number. 'Please, when will it be convenient to come and see your leotard? No – it's not for me, it's for my wife.'

There's good grazing for the imaginative eye around the pastures of the old cork board. 'Ladies', for example, are 'required for Carnation Nursery. 35p per hour. 46p weekends.' Nursing carnations presumably offers warm, soothing fragrance as payment in kind above the paltry payment in cash. 'Set of drain rods wanted, fair price if in fair condition', argues quite a different aspect of the fragrance trade. Never having owned drain rods, but always managed to borrow them from a neighbourly source sets me worrying a bit. Are my accessible drain rods going to vanish into anonymity? Has my neighbour had the tip-off that main drainage is, at *last*, really going to happen within the twelve month? And the rates escalate? Main drainage has been coming 'within the twelve month' for the past seventy two months.

We view upon the cork board so many of the poignant pains and pleasures of parenthood. 'Help for Mother with First Baby' pleads this one, while just below it Junior is well out of rompers and Tiny Tot dungarees, for 'Large Climbing Frame for Sale'. Junior has outgrown his climbing frame, but, ah! the echoes of that radiant faraway moment when the climbing frame was brought triumphantly home, smelling lacquer-new and set up in the garden. 'Oh, how he'll love it, Fred – worth every penny of the money'. Junior's off to school. Maybe 'Mother with First Baby' should make a forward-looking investment.

The notice offering two bunk beds for £6 and four deck chairs for £1.50 had the bunk beds scratched out in forty eight hours in September. But nobody in January, it seems, wants those sleazy old deck chairs even at around 35p apiece. They're *not* a very beguiling buy are used deck chairs in mid-winter!

A 'Pine Chest of Drawers' sounds reasonable enough at £8. One knows the citizen offering them. If he's been able to afford that new streamlined kitchen extension, perhaps he'll take £6? Let it pass, let it pass. The Pine Chest of Drawers probably will before I've done my sums.

'Navy White Pedigree Pram £8' makes it abundantly clear that the couple in 'Pear Trees' have decided to have no truck with the population explosion, and have settled for the Pill in perpetuum. Pity, really. Why not a pigeon pair, a sister, maybe, for that jolly little chap Daniel? But, let's face it, that's their business, even if they have proclaimed it publicly for all the Parish to see. Therein lies the human delight of reading the gossip column of the old cork board.

We've often speculated about the identity of that pallid young man with the shoulder-length ginger hair, turtle neck and jeans seen quietly bicycling sometimes up and sometimes down the road to Gosling Green. Who is he? Where does he live? What's he doing here? At last we know. Or deduce that we do.

'Simple lodging required', reads the notice, 'for quiet, respectable 18 year old Apprentice.'

But of course – that small new woodwork outfit at Gosling Green. It is satisfying to know that our ginger-haired cyclist is not a drop-out wheeling from trip to trip, but a sober young craftsman bent on a seriously unbent two-way trip, morning and evening. Quietly and respectably.

What a pity, in a way, that he does not serve his quiet and respectable apprenticeship in Siblingham, twenty miles away, and abandon that wet, wintering bicycle for this: 'Lift offered Siblingham daily, leaving 8 a.m. Leave Siblingham 17 Hours. £1 p.w.' 20p a day door to door seems a cut rate fare to be grabbed. Nice work for the advertiser, too, for a trouble-free weekend bottle of Cyprus Sherry and a pint of bitter at *The Star*.

Help! Help! Help! wail the cards on the old cork board. Daily Help, Morning Help, Any Old Help, including Baby Sitting Help. 'Reliable Woman Required – 9 to 12.' Imagination takes off, but it's less suspect than 21 to 24. The very upper-crust Lady who came a year ago to live in style at the Queen Anne house named Fawcett's Grange has, not surprisingly, and so far as one knows, been Helpless since her arrival. She certainly didn't know *our* Parish when she pinned a card to the board reading: 'Daily Charwoman Urgently Needed. Hard Worker Essential.'

Our local ladies are proud persons, living in the twentieth, and not the nineteenth century. Charwoman, indeed! Who does she think *she* is?

I do not know what a 'Fold Unit for Poultry' actually is, though guess it to be some kind of chicken container. The mind returns to a laneside notice of ineffable charm seen during the summer in South-West Scotland. 'Beware', it warned, 'Brown Hens Crossing'. What rich, orange-dark yolks these crossing hens suggested and might not the cautious owner be advised to buy a job lot of Poultry Fold Units from his own McFerguson's Post Office Stores?

I may, given world enough, cash and time, make many parishioners if not myself, well content by purchasing a 22-inch-chest child's Anorak, a worn-out Triang Rocker, a limed oak tea trolley (£3 or near offer) and a Thor Washer, whatever a Thor Washer may be. There's a two-bar Electric Fire on offer, too, and four hundred feet of elderly chestnut paling.

Last, and most deeply speculative of all, comes 'Bathroom Scales Very Cheap'. Surely, surely, these may belong to the lady of the cast off leotard who has cast off all the neurotic botheration of weight and diet and returned to a carefree comradeship with cream cakes.